ZOMBIES IN
WESTERN CULTURE

Zombies in Western Culture

A Twenty-First Century Crisis

John Vervaeke, Christopher Mastropietro,
and Filip Miscevic

OpenBook Publishers

https://www.openbookpublishers.com

© 2017 John Vervaeke, Christopher Mastropietro and Filip Miscevic.

All external links were active at the time of publication unless otherwise stated and have been archived via the Internet Archive Wayback Machine at https://archive.org/web

Digital material and resources associated with this volume are available at https://www.openbookpublishers.com/product/602#resources

Every effort has been made to identify and contact copyright holders and any omission or error will be corrected if notification is made to the publisher.

ISBN Paperback: 9781783743285
ISBN Hardback: 9781783743292
ISBN Digital (PDF): 9781783743308
ISBN Digital ebook (epub): 9781783743315
ISBN Digital ebook (mobi): 9781783743322
DOI: 10.11647/OBP.0113

Cover image: *Zombies* (2013), by Benjamin Réthoré. CC BY 2.0, https://www.flickr.com/photos/bnthor/32590607323/in/photostream/

All paper used by Open Book Publishers is SFI (Sustainable Forestry Initiative), PEFC (Programme for the Endorsement of Forest Certification Schemes) and Forest Stewardship Council(r)(FSC(r) certified.

Printed in the United Kingdom, United States, and Australia
by Lightning Source for Open Book Publishers (Cambridge, UK)

Contents

Authors

Dr. John Vervaeke is an Assistant Professor, in the teaching stream. He has been teaching at the University of Toronto since 1994. He currently teaches courses in the Psychology Department and the Cognitive Science Program. He has won and been nominated for several teaching awards including the 2001 Students' Administrative Council and Association of Part-time Undergraduate Students Teaching Award for the Humanities, and the 2012 Ranjini Ghosh Excellence in Teaching Award. He has published articles on relevance realization, general intelligence, mindfulness, metaphor, and wisdom. His abiding passion is to address the Meaning Crisis that besets western culture.

Christopher Mastropietro has completed a BA in semiotics, philosophy and political science at the University of Toronto. He has been working with John Vervaeke since 2012 to formulate and publish a response to the western Meaning Crisis with convergent insights from cognitive science, philosophy and other disciplines. Christopher is interested in the interaction between sacred symbols and wisdom, and the emergence of identity within interpersonal relationships.

Filip Miscevic is currently a Ph.D. student in the Cognitive Science Program at Indiana University Bloomington, studying under Dr. Olaf Sporns in the Computational Cognitive Neuroscience Laboratory. He completed a BSc in cognitive science, neuroscience and computer science at the University of Toronto in 2015, where he was a student of John Vervaeke. He is fascinated by how an understanding of the mind will revolutionize not only our clinical and scientific practices, but our social and cultural ones as well—and in particular how it will come to bear on the Meaning Crisis discussed in this book, for which the zombie has become the flag-bearer.

Acknowledgements

The authors gratefully acknowledge the contributions of the following people, whose feedback helped to focus and refine the arguments in this book: Sean al-Baroudi, Sara Hansen, Scott Gardiner, Sasa Milic, Kelly Mudie, Amogh Sahu and Anderson Todd. We also thank Alessandra Tosi for her excellent feedback and collaboration.

1. A New Zeitgeist

"Not the Black Death, this time; the Gray Life".
Huxley 1962: 59

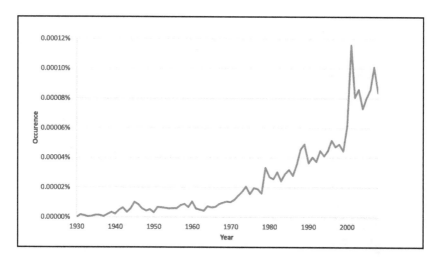

Fig. 1: Prevalence of the use of the word "zombie" from 1920–2008 in predominantly English books published in any country.[1]

Fig. 2: *Zombie Walk Mexico* (2011). Photo by Munir Hamdan.[2]

---

1   From Google N-Gram Viewer (Michel et al. 2011).
2   Flickr, CC BY 2.0, https://bit.ly/2pcvULo

In 2001, a very peculiar performance art begins to take place across North America. It occurs first in Sacramento, California and again two years later in Toronto, Ontario. By 2008, it starts recurring annually in certain urban centers, grows steadily with each passing year, and spreads from one city to the next. Sometimes it has fewer than 50 participants. Sometimes it has over 1000. In late 2011, Mexico City boasts a record of 9,000. Some gatherings are meticulous and coordinated, others are impromptu. Some participants join in advance, and many decide to follow spontaneously. Before long, the phenomenon begins to spread around the globe.

Fig. 3: "I thought that beauty alone would satisfy. But the soul is gone. I can't bear those empty, staring eyes". Screenshot from the Halperin brothers' 1932 film, *White Zombie*, at 40:11.[3]

It should surprise us that these "walks" have only begun to appear, when the paradigm for their behavior has existed since the Halperin brothers produced *White Zombie* in 1932. In this film, a young man turned voodoo master transforms a young woman into a subordinate, pale-skinned corpse. Though his motive is initially to gain her love, his magic succeeds only in removing her vitality. This ironic consequence comes to effect change in his intentions, and he repents to her: "I thought that beauty alone would satisfy. But the soul is gone. I can't bear those empty, staring eyes". It is a mark of how the zombie has developed over the years that the word "beauty" could ever have been used to describe it.

---

3   A remastered version of the movie is available at https://www.youtube.com/watch?v=lQ0hL4EBC58

The outbreak of zombieism is a twentieth century phenomenon, but in the twenty-first century it explodes into zeitgeist. Over 600 zombie movies have been made since 1920, but over one half of them have been in the last 10 years. Two great waves have lapped onto the shore of American cinema since 2000: one around 2001, and then again in 2008.[4] *Twenty-Eight Days Later* comes out in 2002, George Romero's *Dawn of the Dead* is remade in 2004, and *Zombieland* becomes the highest-grossing zombie film to date in 2009. This is quickly overtaken in 2013, first by *Warm Bodies*, and then by the Brad Pitt epic, *World War Z*.[5] By 2015, there are three TV series based on zombies: *Z Nation* on Netflix, *iZombie* on CW, and AMC's breakthrough hit, *The Walking Dead*.[6] The genre has also enjoyed considerable success in the medium of video games, most notably in the highly lauded *The Last of Us*.[7]

Clearly, the zombie has transcended the constraints of its own genre. Whereas early zombie films closely adhered to horror tropes, more recent renditions have wed themselves to comedy and romance (Zack Snyder released the comedic Shaun of the Dead in 2004 to critical and popular acclaim),[8] and broken away from melodrama. The zombie has become a pervasive cultural symbol that is constantly expanding its reference, not content to relegate itself to its tradition. As Deleuze and Guattari (1972: 332) put it "the only modern myth is the myth of zombies". The zombie seems to be a shifting signifier with an unending hermeneutical compass. And yet its features remain remarkably consistent from one story to the next, and it has represented many varieties of apocalypse without altering its basic nature: consumerism, poverty, hunger, political dystopia and

---

4   Annalee Newitz (2008), "War and Social Upheaval Cause Spikes in Zombie Movie Production", i09.com

5   Trailers available on YouTube: *Twenty-Eight Days Later* at https://www.youtube.com/watch?v=c7ynwAgQlDQ; *Dawn of the Dead* at https://www.youtube.com/watch?v=-IIwV_Y6VU; *Zombieland* at https://www.youtube.com/watch?v=8m9EVP8X7N8; *Warm Bodies* at https://www.youtube.com/watch?v=yvjwKqA2_9U; World War Z at https://www.youtube.com/watch?v=HcwTxRuq-uk

6   Trailers are available on YouTube: *Z Nation* at https://www.youtube.com/watch?v=7ZFIS2AqAz8; *iZombie* (Season 1) at https://www.youtube.com/watch?v=UndyIFo_jZ4; *The Walking Dead* (Season 1) at https://www.youtube.com/watch?v=sfAc2U20uyg

7   The trailer of *The Last of Us* is available on YouTube at https://www.youtube.com/watch?v=OQWD5W3fpPM

8   The trailer of *Shaun of the Dead* is available on YouTube at https://www.youtube.com/watch?v=LIfcaZ4pC-4

environmental degradation, zombies have assumed a heterogeneity of ugliness. No longer simply a vehicle for entertainment, it has become the basis for critical reflection and cultural self-examination, to which an increasing number of academic publications on the subject attest (Goto-Jones 2015; Moreman 2010; Webb and Byrnand 2008). For instance, Television Ontario devoted an episode of The Agenda with Steve Paikin in 2011 to an unreserved examination of humanity's most nauseating adversary. Four panelists—Daniel Drezner, Arnold T. Blumberg, Robert Smith and Andrew Watson—sat down to parse its menaces and flesh out its metaphors. Zombies have pressed us with the dangers of a unique moment in time, and they have become the most enduring, expressive and consummate metaphor for our crisis in meaning.

The zombie has been subject to a vast variety of interpretations by culture theorists and academics. To examine these exhaustively would be beyond the scope of this or any other monograph. The affinity between zombies and states of human decrepitude has permitted the view that zombies can stand for nearly every conceivable human failing. The present authors propose that the interpretations most favoured by academics—mortality, consumerism and environmental degradation among them—are plausible without being sufficient. The mere fact that each seems to apply invalidates the proposition that any one of them can apply exclusively. We take the position that this exegetic pigeonholing often falls deftly into the "forest for the trees" category of thinking. The zombie zeitgeist accommodates interpretations of disquiet about many topics, yet we will argue that each of these readings should be understood as elements of a broader symptomatology. This symptomatology, we will explain, relates to a condition that is far more complex than has been supposed by any theorist that has previously written on this topic.

We propose that the cultural phenomenon of the zombie has provided us with a constellation of four intersecting symbols for a modern human ethos, and that these symbols represent a crisis of worldview that has no precedent in modern western civilization. Our use of the collective pronoun "we" shall be in broad reference to North-American and Western culture more generally. This limitation notwithstanding, the authors will make no claims regarding the applicability of these arguments to cultures that may fall outside of that moniker.[9]

In this book we will suggest that the appearance of these zombie symbols is approximately co-emergent with the West's dawning cultural awareness of a worldview crisis, and that there are sufficient correlations between the traits of the zombie and the symptomology of the crisis to demonstrate this linkage reliably. We will provide a preliminary discussion of the origins of the crisis (the full argument will be reserved for forthcoming work), and argue that it is extant in the personal, social, political and religious domains of life in which we participate, and which define us uniquely as a meaning-making species.

In the forthcoming sections, we will also argue that while the zombie is a versatile enough symbol to stand for many kinds of human defilement, the symbol ultimately draws its aptness from being a perversion of the Christian mythos of death and resurrection, and that most of its traits and features have emerged from, and harken back to, the matrix of the Christian worldview. We will contend that the zombie has evolved to become a representation of the loss of the sacred canopy traditionally provided by Christianity, and that its features have evolved along the fault lines of this loss, representing a world that no longer explains itself, nor provides us instruction for how to live within it.

Section 2 will retrace the genealogy of the zombie from its precursory influences and the peak popularity that began at the turn of this century. We will also discuss how the zombie replaced the extra-terrestrials to become the preeminent monster for the twenty-first century, reflecting the weariness and alienation left by the Cold War and the threat of nuclear apocalypse.

Section 3 will provide the main exegesis of the zombie itself, separating its myth into four predominant symbols that are recurrent in its popular depictions in film, television, and other literature. These symbols will not simply be icons associated with the zombie's image;

---

9   It will be apparent throughout the monograph that our reference to 'the West' is invoked with predominantly American examples. As the US is the most significant exporter of popular culture in the West, our focus on American culture is proportionate to its contribution to the phenomenon. Though this does not necessarily suggest that the phenomenon is absent from other western countries, America certainly seems to be the epicenter of the crisis, and most exemplary of its features.

they will be the zombie's physical attributes, the treatment of its name, contortions of its narrative structure and the ecology of apocalypse that invariably follows it from one story to the next.

Section 4 will introduce the concept of cultural domicide (the destruction of home) by exploring two chronologically distant but revealing case studies examining the loss of home on a cultural scale. The first of these will refer the Grassy Narrows First Nation in Ontario, Canada, and the second to the decline of the Hellenistic civilization following the death of Alexander the Great in 323 BCE. This section will depart from discussions of the zombie to build a framework for worldview attunement that will inform the discussions in the remaining sections.

Section 5 will discuss the symptomatology of this crisis in detail using the four horsemen of the Christian apocalypse as an analogue for the four domains affected by the meaning crisis. Famine, Pestilence, War and Death will stand for the personal, social, political and religious manifestations of the crisis, framed by the loss of worldview introduced in the previous section.

Section 6 will offer an overview of the historical origins of the meaning crisis, tracing the rise and fall of a western worldview that was composed of three constellating orders from the Aristotelean and Christian paradigms. This introductory genealogy will chronicle the emergence of our cultural domicide throughout the centuries, an argument that will be elaborated in forthcoming work.

Though we will subdivide the representational corpus of the zombie zeitgeist into different symbols in section 3, and the symptoms in section 5, we will also refer to the amalgam of zombie phenomena as a single symbol for the purpose of surveying these phenomena collectively. There are two fundamental claims that we will introduce hereto and reiterate throughout this book. The first is that, by almost all accounts, zombies are the fictionally distorted, self-reflected image of modern humanity. Most zombie interpretations begin with this premise, that in some pivotal way, "zombies are us" (see e.g., Goto-Jones 2015, Moreman 2010, Webb and Byrnand 2008). This book will seek to add valence and depth to this proposition. Zombies do represent us, but more specifically, they represent the ruin of all that is meaningful within us. Zombies represent the modern deterioration of our uniquely human ability to make and sustain meaning in our lives.

The second conclusion is that the zombie zeitgeist is a powerful but inarticulate form of representation. It is a raw opus of pop art, and it is not replete with self-analysis. The main function of zombie symbol seems to *express* the meaning crisis, not to treat or explain it. Naturally then, our aim here is to buffer the gaps within the zombie's expression with the evaluation required to appreciate its gravity. This is our undertaking in the forthcoming sections.

2. A Transition in Metaphors: A Brief History of Monster Zeitgeists

We are surrounded by strangers. But for stretches of our history, strangers have not been as strange as they are now. There have been epochs of culture when we have sustained a concerted frame of reference that made us known and knowable to one another wherever we lived. Even when we shared very little, we could be sure to find some universal commons that would guarantee us familiarity with an unfamiliar person. For much of our recent past, we in the West lived all under the canopy of Christendom. However varied or populated our society was, other human beings always offered a degree of predictability as long as they identified *as* Christians. We could always anticipate a median grade of behavior, and presuppose binary limits on a spectrum between the sacred and the profane.[1] Sustaining our religious commons was not as much about celebrating common principles as much as it was about extending our scope of acquaintance. The "extended family" metaphors used in religious discourse were very provident in fostering this acquaintance. Strangeness was never absolute strangeness, and we could find others intelligible to the degree that they assured a comprehensible—if not always amiable—interaction. More contemporary cultural canopies came in the form of ethnic or civic membership, but because citizenship

---

1   We are not implying that these expectations were qualified, or that everyone did in fact adhere to a certain standard of virtue. What we are referring to is merely the perception of this standard, not its reality.

    https://doi.org/10.11647/OBP.0113.02

and ethnicity are often more involuntary, they are not as grounded in principled participation. They are not as comprehensively penetrating, and therefore less powerful than religious bonds. Thus, they are much more susceptible to the vicissitudes of political and economic change. One of the more puissant cultural canopies in the twentieth century was the phenomenon of "Americanism". Particularly in the latter half of the century, being American connoted a strong apotheosis of values and perspective for most Americans. In most cases, if two Americans had diverging interests, backgrounds or orientations, they could be sure to touch base on certain convictions held mutually fundamental. Significantly, many attribute the vitality of Americanness to the influence of a vernacular religiosity—the "faith in America".

Yet, as Dreyfus and Kelly (2011) observe, we no longer share a uniform worldview that guarantees agreement on sacredness or standards of behavior. We are talking about a changing worldview, rather than a single event or moment in history. This has been a gradual process. Now, the powerful twentieth century "Americanism" is nearly a misnomer; two persons can share its title and share almost nothing else. The alienation we feel in everyday life suggests that experiences of foreignness—exposure to "otherness" of persons or place—are becoming inherent in domestic life. This dovetails with burgeoning literature discussing the disintegration of social candor, "common courtesy" and the sense of locality that made America perceive itself as a neighborhood of frankness and fluid exchange. Public intimacy is what is at stake, the feeling of recognition; understanding, and being understood, by other human beings.

Zombies are not the first monsters to broach this theme. By and large, they have taken over from a villain H. G. Wells introduced in his 1898 novel *War of the Worlds* that has inspired numerous film adaptations since its original publication.[2] Extra-terrestrial invasions gained tremendous popularity in American cinema, particularly in the latter half of the twentieth century with the onset of the Cold War. As the West drew its cultural boundaries more guardedly, the alien seemed to be an effective mask for the prevailing wind of wariness and paranoia, and the fear of outsiders and espionage. Stories of alien invasion struck compelling

---

2   The trailer of *War of the Worlds* is available on YouTube at https://www.youtube. com/results?search_query=war+of+the+worlds+trailer

affinities with real-life suspicions: adversaries from the outside were trying to infiltrate our society in order to advance theirs, to dissolve our systems and propagate their own, and to estrange us from one another by diluting our fellowship. These suspicions were significant in that they inadvertently discouraged intimacy; people were not guaranteed to be trustworthy, many were not who they said they were, and it was difficult to gauge a stranger's memberships and commitments. It was possible that your new friend was not the "American" she said she was, and that she had come under the canopy to sabotage its integrity. One of the most dramatic fictionalizations of this kind of mania was depicted in a famous episode of *The Twilight Zone*,[3] where a few well-disguised aliens interfered with technology to cause an outbreak of disquiet on an American residential street, engendering enmity between neighbors in order to weaken their awareness of a coming invasion.

Zombies take up many of these traits, but they make some significant departures fit for a post-Cold War, post-globalized, post-Christian and (as some people say) post-modern world. The first evident difference is that zombies don't trouble to conceal their invasion. It wouldn't occur to them. And unlike most diabolical, imperial alien overlords, zombies don't have a reason for invading in the first place.

---

3   The episode *The Monsters Are Due on Maple Street* is available on YouTube at https://www.youtube.com/watch?v=g7OGCe08eXo

3. The Four Symbols of the Zombie Metaphor

Following Christopher Moreman, we note that while there has been much academic discussion of zombie movies, there has been little examination of the zombie itself, prompting us to "analyze the zombie as a symbol in itself" (Moreman 2010: 264). Motivation is not all that the zombie lacks. As a symbol of the loss of meaning, the zombie embodies a plethora of vacancies, empty placeholders for the building blocks of meaning.

3.1 The First Symbol: The Semiosis of the Zombie

1. *Zombies don't talk.*

They aren't mute or reticent. They simply have no language. They have nothing to say. They don't transmit gists of conversation. Crucially, they do the opposite: they transmit their own vacuity. They communicate their incommunicability. The zombie's most marked pathology is that it lacks intelligibility.

2. *Zombies are communal.*

With a twist: they possess the momentum and self-organization of culture, without the narrative imagination that gathers common purpose. Hence, zombies are like culture gone awry. They are communal creatures in that they vaguely share proximity, but there is no accord among them (see also Webb and Byrnand 2008). They cannot read in or reach out to one another. They do not coordinate to achieve concurrence.

They are in company, but not together. They are surrounded, but each alone. They lack culture.

3. *Zombies are homeless.*

Zombies do not have lairs, nests, coffins, castles or caves. They do not retreat anywhere as sun breaks the horizon, as the moon breaks the clouds or as the spring breaks the winter. Zombies drift. They are equally suited, and unsuited, to the ground they occupy. They do not have province in any one space (see also Webb and Byrnand 2008). They do not have propriety for any one person. There is nothing whatsoever about a zombie that appears to belong to the world. A zombie simply "shuffles", bungles absently from one place to the next. If zombies were human, they might be feeling a little uprooted. But perhaps we can understand a portion of their plight. Not belonging anywhere, being from anywhere... this is precisely part of the encroaching foreignness we described in section 2. Zombies lack home.

4. *Zombies eat brains.*

The appetite of a zombie is a very particular kind of appetite. No matter how much a zombie devours, it will continue feeding for as long as it is able. Its gormandizing is indiscriminate and voracious, and its famishment apparently bottomless. But it is insubstantial. The zombie represents raw consumption. It does not seem to imbibe the things it consumes; it simply extinguishes them. A zombie never stops eating, but never grows or changes. In its insatiability, the zombie has put its face to the disorder of addiction. It craves with absolute singularity, and its craving becomes its nature. It wants to have, but never to be (see also Fromm 1976). It is constantly filling, but never gets full. The zombie's lack has become a hunger (see also Webb and Byrnand 2008). In fact, in one pivotal scene[1] in *Day of the Dead*,

> the pointlessness of the zombie appetite [is made apparent] as one captured zombie continues to try to eat despite the fact that its internal organs have been removed and so the "food" simply drops to the floor upon being swallowed. (Moreman 2010: 275)

---

1   Scene available at https://gomovies.to/film/day-of-the-dead-1985-17728/watching.html?ep=549712 at 22:57.

Zombies are a brain-oriented monster, in operation, appetite and vulnerability. Interestingly, in many accounts of the zombie, the only way to kill a zombie is by destroying its brain—if you will: obliterating mind to obliterate mindlessness. We can find a strange twist tucked into this pattern: that the mindlessness evinced by the zombie is begotten by its brain. Zombies are a perversion of mind precisely because they notably lack the properties of mind we think fundamentally human, yet they visibly want to acquire mind in the most literal sense of acquisition. Only by destroying their brains do you destroy the threat to your brains posed by their mindlessness. What is being intimated here is a very unsettling dependency between the threat of mindlessness and the possessing of mind. The brain is a symbol for intelligibility. The devouring of the brain indicates the devouring of that intelligibility and all it affords. The fact that brain is driving the consumption of brain is a deeply complex symbolic occurrence; culture is devouring culture, mind is devouring mind, humanness is devouring humanness. This evinces a deep presence of mindlessness within mind. Implicitly, it tells us that zombies are not an external threat, but an internal one. They are a symbolic villain that assumes most characteristics of humanity, and subverts them with decay. As one character in *The Walking Dead* points out to his fellow survivors:[2] *"We* are the walking dead" (see also Goto-Jones 2015; Moreman 2010; Webb and Byrnand 2008).

5. *Zombies are ugly.*

This is the operative difference between the zombie and most other popular horrors. Vampires are flushed with sex appeal, Frankenstein's monster is endearing, and in its exotic way, even the werewolf is a beauteous animal. But zombies are ugly by definition: dead, rotting, stinking, without vitals, lacking the spirit that makes one human being attractive to another. A zombie is not guilty of concealment or duplicity. The ugly mug does not sheath any hidden depths. The essence of a zombie shares the visage of its appearance. Ugliness is the zombie's nature. We cannot see the mind of a zombie because they have no mind to see. The vacancy in a zombie's gaze provides a window to the absence of soul.

---

2   Season 5, episode 10 is available on YouTube at https://www.youtube.com/watch?v=AyYuvILOgck

The enduring disconcertment is the fact that zombies look like us. They do not just happen to look like us; therein froths the real potency of the metaphor. Zombies are something inhuman in human form—not just ugly, but ugly in the image of person. Dehumanization makes the zombie more destitute than the ugliest orc, that they are a debasement of cosmetic sensibilities. And the zombie upends all cosmos in human nature. Physical ugliness is its deformity of dignity. Mindlessness is deformity of the intelligible. The human guise of a zombie aborts human feeling. It reviles contact. It brings us to a dead end.

6. *Zombies are not evil.*

Unlike the conspiring alien, the deceptive vampire, or the malevolent spirit, the zombie lacks the defining characteristic of monstrous villainy: it lacks evil. Because of its mindlessness, the zombie does not possess malevolence; even as it drags itself forward in consumption, it is merely scrabbling to satisfy a base instinct of its own craving. But it does not do so with the awareness of malintent. The destructiveness of the zombie's impact is no more known to it than a bacterial infection is known to the culpable bacteria. The zombie, dangerous, hideous and destructive though it is, intuitively defies the category of evil. Despite the twisted resemblance to its living counterpart, the zombie is no more evil than a rabid animal.

7. *Zombies are heedless.*

Zombies are fierce and threatening, but not self-preserving. They give no thought to defending themselves against harm. In this sense, they lack the defining feature of a living organism. They bear no fundamental relationship to their survival. In pursuit of consumption they will destroy themselves (see also Webb and Byrnand 2008).

8. *Zombies are untouchable.*

Their ugliness is catchable, and they have a 100% rate of contagion. If you come into contact with a zombie, infection follows inevitably. We don't want to be ugly, mindless, homeless or incommunicable, so when confronted with a zombie, we take care to keep our distance. But the deprivation of closeness is severely consequential. If we are to suppose that the monster really has been created in our image, then it poses several complications to our yen for touch.

Our penchant for touch is, ultimately, what distinguishes intimate relationships from non-intimate ones, not only relationships with people, but with animals, objects, and concepts. The more "in touch" we are with something, the closer and more connected we are to that thing. Touch is the medium of intimacy. Without it, it is hard to imagine that intimacy could exist at all. However, intimacy is not the only casualty of the zombie's untouchableness.

Our being in the world is heavily dependent upon touch to keep a continuity of contact with our surroundings. Experience is deemed "true" when it *impresses* us through contact. We come to believe something as a result of having touched it, literally or otherwise. We come to be affected by it once it has "touched us" in turn. And of course, we don't consider our relationships to be loving relationships until we feel comfortable with touching one another.

Touch is the arbiter of "real". Assertions of verity are always made with permutations of a touch metaphor. Those with whom we are intimate are more real to us. Objects we have *handled* are more real to us. Emotions we have *felt* are more real to us. Losing touch costs us our grasp on reality.

3.1.1 Intensifying Meaninglessness: Zombies as a Threat to the Three Marks of Realness

Realness is a multivalent term. Conversationally, it is often used in reference to qualities of lucidity that are not captured by its ontological definition, which refers strictly to truth and falsehood. When an individual says that something feels "real" she is seldom referring to whether something is verifiable. Instead, she refers to a sense of connection, a way in which her felt experience relates to patterns or events in the world. This relating is often described with reference to propositions of truth and falseness, but this is only a reference in metaphor. A "sense of realness" is a psychological experience, not a metaphysical principle.

Our sense of touch is an apt analogue for this psychological experience, and the symbol of the zombie has appropriated it. The contact implied by touch represents a quality of relation that is integral to feelings of connection; meaning. Metaphorically, touch is a versatile enough source domain to represent both cerebral and physical forms of relating. The zombie co-opts this versatility. The felt sense of realness is not a single impression, but a series of marks that relate to (i) the intelligible, (ii) the interactional, the (iii) interior and (iv) the insight-affording connections that orient our actions in the world. The nature of the zombie undermines each of these marks. It poses a paradox that undercuts intelligibility, it has an inter-categorical nature that confuses our interaction, it vacuums our interior presence of mind, and it bankrupts us of a promised capacity to use insight to transcend the boundaries of outmoded perspectives. We will discuss the first three marks in this section, and the fourth in section 3.4.1.

3.1.1.1 The Zombie is Paradoxical; It Defies Intelligibility

Intelligibility as an explicitly discussed concept began in many ways with Plato's dialogues. It refers to the rational confirmation of reality and its contents, the form in which the world is represented reflectively in human cognition. To the degree that our minds grasp the form of something, can identify it notionally based on distinguishable properties, we would say that the thing is intelligible; readable by our minds.

The zombie defies rational confirmation because it lacks the coherence of properties that allow us to form rational definitions. The nature of the zombie is beset by paradox; it is human and non-human, living and not living, cultural and non-cultural, natural and supernatural, suspended between fundamental binaries that most definitions presuppose.

Living ———————— [zombie] ———————— Non-living

The zombie not only eludes a definition of its own, it also disrupts the definitional integrity maintained by the binaries it is suspended between: if the zombie is both alive and not alive, what now does it mean to be "alive"? And if it is both human and non-human, what then does it mean to be "human"?

Human ——————— [zombie] ——————— Non-human

Intelligibility allows us to see the world with conceptual clarity. The definition of the zombie is unintelligible, which means that any likeness associated with the zombie is distorted by that association, like an image that has come too near the fracture line of a broken mirror. The contradictions of the zombie provoke a disconfirmation, a kind of black hole within its intelligibility that vacuums any elements that have been tethered to its likeness, including and especially its humanity. The zombie's influence disrupts the binary relationship of the human and non-human. This raises the question "what is the difference between the human and the zombie?" Our sense of realness in our humanity can quickly be destabilized by the zombie's presence.

The zombie paradox is not just problematic from the safety of its fiction. The zombie is very nearly human, enough to be a moniker for certain human states and behaviors. Consider, for example, how frequently we use "zombie" to describe stupors of illness, fatigue or mental dysfunction, and consider the similarities to the destitution of the monster. Like the alien, the zombie walks a line between natural and supernatural, and our incredulousness toward it seems tentative enough for the monster to be hypothesized as a genuine biological terror. Therefore, the paradox of the zombie not only rests upon the question "is it human?" but also upon the question "does it exist at all?"

This paradox is the prime potency of the zeitgeist, the axle upon which all other symbols of the zombie rotate. The likeness and unlikeness to humanness are both uncanny. The zombie is not only a paradox by definition (or lack thereof), but also in its epistemological intrusiveness: the monster cannot be disconfirmed. We cannot be sure that such a thing exists, or does not exist. Moreover, if it does exist, we cannot be sure it is not simply ourselves, a distorted reflection in the pond on the other side of the non-human spectrum. The paradox of the zombie defies the intelligible. It defies a consistent, conceptual sense of realness.

3.1.1.2 The Zombie is Inter-categorical; It Defies Interaction

The zombie's paradoxical place on the spectrum between human and non-human, existent and non-existent, and natural and supernatural, undermines a second mark of realness. The zombie is an inter-categorical monster—it is perpetually in-between categories, neither one thing nor its opposite. Intelligibility is required for rational confirmation, but for something to seem real, representation is not sufficient. Simply put: we need to know what things are so that we know how to encounter them.

We need to be able to place them before us. There is a sensual dimension to realness. Understanding is not enough; we need to be able to interact with the world.

The kind of contact provided by interaction is not an intellectual kind, but the kind that relates to action. The sense of realness is an embodied sense, not simply a cerebral one. The world must not only make sense, it must have sense. It must not only be represented, it must also be reciprocated. It must be touchable, and it must touch us in turn.

This is where the inter-categorical nature of the zombie interferes with our sense of realness: it encumbers our ability to interact. We noted in the previous section that contagion is among the zombie's more salient features, and within the monster's narrative, survivors who encounter a zombie must avoid touching it at all costs. The more multitudinous the zombies become, the more this danger is compounded. In a world inhabited by the zombie, the physicality of touch becomes an undying hazard. Ordinary humans are constantly at risk of exposure, and are therefore zombies in waiting. This is a world that discourages contact in all of its forms and bucks the rituals of interaction. For this reason, the zombie represents a crisis of intimacy. We treat everyone like a stranger in this world because it is the only way to avoid infection. In this world, we are surrounded and yet stranded, inundated while utterly alone. This simultaneity of the zombie's presence and absence is an inter-categorical problem laid over the paradox of its unintelligible definition. Not only is the zombie—and by extension, its human foils—unclear and disconfirming, it is also profoundly alienating.

3.1.1.3 The Zombie is Vacant; It Lacks Interiority

Of the many paradigmatic influences that have trained our sense of realness, Cartesian has been perhaps the most pivotal. Much of the Western philosophical tradition continues to lean on the metaphysical and epistemological framework laid by Descartes treatises. The *cogito ergo sum* of Descartes' *Meditations* is one of those maxims in Western philosophy distinguished by its rare notoriety; its philosophical import on the question of "what is real?" is still the prime reference for enlightenment philosophy, not just within the annals of academic work, but for the broader culture and its epistemic presuppositions.

The Cartesian tradition sets out the third of our fundamental marks of realness: clear and distinct intellectual perception. At the center of this mark is the phenomenon of metacognition, the mind's ability to recognize and reflect back on itself. This self-recognition of consciousness is the individual's awareness of himself, his existence, and his capacity to think and, therefore, to be. To Descartes, this fundamental criterion was a kind of charter with reality, an ontological base camp from which to brave the wilds of a potentially duplicitous world. The interior of the camp was the individual's certainty of his own realness.

The zombie defies this mark of realness perhaps more obviously than any other, and in so doing it builds upon its paradox from the previous marks. A lack of human consciousness is definitive of the zombie, particularly because it is otherwise so strikingly human in appearance. It is because of this trait more than any other that the zombie becomes the source domain for human debasement—the literal lack of consciousness is a symbol for states of mental absence, fugue and fatigue that have become idiomatically synonymous with zombification. The most common reason we refer to someone as a zombie is that he doesn't seem fully conscious. He is not aware of himself. He does not notice the world go by.

The zombie lacks an inner life, an interior presence of mind that is commensurate with thought, intention and direction. The zombie's inner vacancy is symbolized by a blank stare and shifting movement, driven by unreflective, sub-human cravings. The lack of interiority means that the zombie cannot connect to the world, it cannot affirm its own realness by the Cartesian criterion, and it cannot affirm the realness of its environment. Turned on the individual, this lack is wholly destructive. Her connection with the world is severed at the stem, and she cannot even be sure of herself, let alone a world beyond her. An existence without interiority is a disconfirmed existence. It lacks even the most basic constituents on which to build the foundation for a sense of realness.

It is important to understand that the zombie symbolically undermines each of these marks of realness. The zombie is a participatory symbol. By this we mean it invokes and invites action. It does not simply refer to but also instantiates the object of its reference, whether the object is paradox, destitution, homelessness or alienation. A participatory symbol is more active than a regular symbol; a valentine heart and a kiss are both common symbols for love, yet the shape of a valentine heart plays no causal role in love itself, whereas a kiss instigates intimacy. Similarly, the zombie is a participatory symbol because it enacts the phenomenon to which it refers. It does not only stand in for these degenerations, it also demonstrates them. In our own enactments, we in turn demonstrate the zombie.

Activities like the urban zombie walks speak to all that is participatory about the zombie symbol. The simulations in which humans deliberately undermine their own humanity add salience to the zombie's defiance of realness. While such playacting may be dismissed as frivolous, it is also possible that these acts are trying to draw attention to a resemblance. When we take our attention away from the mindless walkers long enough to look around at their human counterparts, we are perhaps meant to genuinely wonder the difference.

3.2 The Second Symbol: The Name of the Zombie

This brings us to our next observation of zombies in popular fiction, though in fact it is more of an observation about our survivors. You may have noticed that zombies are almost never "zombies". No one in film (save the more comedic renderings) ever refers to a zombie as a zombie. They refer to "walkers", "the dead", "the undead", "corpses", "flesh-eaters" or "the infected". But they never use the most common cultural term. In fact, they seem wholly unfamiliar with the concept of a zombie until the apocalypse befalls them. They are ignorant to the tropes associated with the genre of their distress. It is often remarked strange and amusing that no one in a zombie movie—set in the same time and world we live in—seems ever to have seen a zombie movie.

There have been few exceptions to the absence of the term "zombie", but each of these exceptions demonstrates the instability of how the term is used. Once again, even in name the zombies communicate their incommunicability. The first exception is *World War Z*. Uncharacteristically, zombies are here referred to by name, but the characters are quite reluctant to use the term. When they find themselves speaking the name of "zombie" the heroes are ill at ease. Why this reluctance? Traditionally in horror movies, characters are reticent to utter the name of the monster because of the sheer disbelief in supernatural agents. However, coming to believe in the vampire or the werewolf is often the first step in empowering the resistance to the monsters (as soon as the hero knows she is facing a vampire, she knows to arm herself with a crucifix and wooden stake). In contrast, the zombie is not supernatural, nor hard to detect. In *World War Z* (as in most films of the genre) the protagonists are surround by hundreds if not thousands of zombies, so there is no cause for disbelief. Nor does naming the monster provide any empowerment. Absent these traditional reasons, an alternative explanation for the reluctance is needed. Using the term of "zombie" opens a gap in the intelligibility of the world, a vacancy that cannot thereafter be filled. In a traditional horror movie the monster disrupts the order of the characters' world, but in acknowledging the monster's existence, the characters are able to reorder the world to accommodate the supernatural disruption. The evil of the monster becomes a normative guidance; it inspires the effective righteousness of the protagonists. This accommodation is not a passive acquiescence, but an active and effective resistance. The characters can now fight back. However, acknowledging the zombie—who is not evil—brings no accommodation, and yields no empowerment. To use the term is to despair.

Another exception is the film *Only Lovers Left Alive*. It was directed by Jim Jarmusch and released in 2013 to critical acclaim.[3] The film features two centuries' old vampires, Adam and Eve, languishing uneventfully through eternity. When the term "zombie" makes its appearance, it is used not by a human hero, but by one of literature's oldest horror monsters. The vampires use it disdainfully, not in reference to the usual undead creatures, but to ordinary humans. These fanged beings, whose lives appear as meaningless as they are enduring, find the lives of their human contemporaries even more meaningless. Their contempt for our zombie behavior is casual and matter-of-fact. The malaise of human life is, at least to the vampires, an obvious and unquestioned fact. The name of "zombie" is used explicitly and without reluctance only in this case: when it is made to describe human life. *We are the walking dead.*

---

3   A trailer is available on YouTube at https://www.youtube.com/watch?v=ycOKvWrwYFo

When we examine this closely, we begin to realize that the zombie zeitgeist is not a single symbol, but a dynamic constellation of interlocking symbols. The creature of the zombie is the icon of the zeitgeist, and as we have explained, the name of the zombie also carries a symbolic conveyance that embellishes the phenomenon. We might say that these are the first two symbols in the constellation. The next two symbols are more diffuse in their representation. The third symbol is the relation between the viewer and the zombie genre as she encounters it. The fourth symbol is the apocalypse, which is often paired with the zombie, and has given rise the conjoined catchphrase, "zombie apocalypse". Independently and in concert, these symbols speak for the meaning crisis.

3.3 The Third Symbol: The Failure of the Metanarrative

As she follows a story, the viewer integrates two different perspectives in order to gain both involvement and reflection. The viewer has the perspective of the characters in the story, but also a "godlike" perspective beyond that possessed by any character. The relationship between these two perspectives can be called the *metanarrative* of the story. The interplay between these perspectives affords the viewer a kind of participatory insight. This insight in turn inspires a transformation in the viewer. The metanarrative binds the viewer to the meaning of the story. However, in the zombie story there is no transformation. In the zombie story, the two perspectives clash. In the zombie story, the metanarrative fails to bind.

The first stage of any outbreak story is the survivor's struggle to overcome her disorientation and create a profile of her adversary. The viewer's distress of a zombie film is to watch the inevitable unfold— the story begins by focusing on a single character through a window of momentary normalcy. The rising action begins with a very sudden appearance of the outbreak, which the character narrowly manages to escape. After a period of isolation, the character meets other escapees who share information, and the survivors converge on a working perspective of the crisis and their predator. They find some advantageous haven with renewable means of sustenance, and they attempt to fortify it. They delegate roles and try to live as a community.

But it's never to be, because the survivors quarrel. They dissent over trivialities and their tenuous order fails. Conflict divides them into factions, and selfishness breeds mistrust. Usually by some oversight, the wayward survivors alert the zombies to their whereabouts and once again become overrun. Their tentative home disintegrates. They struggle to escape and go on the run, and zombies follow in pursuit. The film reaches its climax as the survivors become desperate and overwhelmed. Most of them fall. The film ends either with the death or infection of the remaining survivors, or with a suggestion of the peril's ceaselessness: that there will only ever be more of the same: fighting... evading... trying to outrun the inevitable (see also Moreman 2010; Webb and Byrnand 2008).

The final revelation of the film extinguishes the last feelings of hope. The survivor feels—as the viewer knows—that there is no land left untouched. There is no one immune from infection. There is no garden to flee to, no island of retreat. There is nowhere left to hide, and there is nothing more to tell. Much like the zombie, the story drifts off as we realize the outbreak is unending. The credits roll ambiguously thereafter.

Stories of the zombie always begin close in and zoom out gradually. We follow a single character as she intakes more and more of her situation's horror. As the camera and story pan, the situation darkens. Chances of survival become less and less likely, and the prospect of salvation becomes bleaker. The story ends as it began, with calamity. But it does not grant us a final understanding. The story ends, but it refuses to conclude.

We watch all of this happen as knowing spectators. We know the walkers are zombies and we know better than to confuse them with humans. We know they eat insatiably and we know they grow in number. We understand the threat before our fictional counterparts experience it, and we look for the firearm long before the survivors acquire it. We anticipate shelter before the survivors find it. We know it will be fruitless as the survivors brace it. We know the survivors will not sustain community. We know the zombies will win by attrition. We know these things as we would of any other fictional horror, but there is a discrepancy in that the survivors know none of it. There is a vast distance between us and the survivors because they are incapable of sharing our references. This is another clue that the human survivors are not quite equal in elevation to the culture that authors them. We know more than they do. We *see* as they do not. Like watching *Oedipus Rex*, we have the expectation of incoming tragedy. We have the feeling of dramatic irony. We can predict the failure of the survivors before they fail.

And yet... it's not really like *Oedipus*. It's not a tragedy. Because while we can predict the survivors' failure, we are no better at understanding it than they are. We certainly cannot predict anything beyond it. And we cannot quite call it ironic either. The absence of a conclusion breaks the pattern that defines dramatic irony, namely comparing the character's apprehensions against the coming of a contrary result. But the zombie has no final result. It has no finality at all. Only drift. Tragedy is marked by a metanarrative, an overseen conclusion that makes sense of the events leading up to it. Metanarratives provide a frame for the story, but the zombie outbreak cannot be framed. We don't know where it has come from, and we don't know where it is going save that it will continue to consume, continue to engulf, delete, and die. Zombies bring not just death, they bring interminable death. The waves of a zombie apocalypse are always falling, without purpose, and without end. Tragedy is an afterword ascribed to events of dramatic suffering, a denouement that dignifies the events of suffering by giving them significance. The zombie apocalypse is the anti-tragedy. It immerses us in a story and denies us closure. It invests us into the face of character and has us look on as the face deforms. It has us watch as the eyes of our protagonists glaze and go blank. It has us hope for the redemption of the human survivors, and ever so slowly, it takes that hope away. The zombie is an aesthetic for the deepest despair because it chokes on a meaningful story. It pushes us into the position of a metanarrative, and then withholds the metanarrative from us.

Even though we identify the tropes, our savvy is otherwise unhelpful because nothing of our irony would assist a survivor in the long run. We can predict the failure of the narrative and the absence of conclusion, but we have nothing to offer in its place. And that, more than anything, is a cause for despair. We cannot transpose ourselves into the crisis and be sure of a more meaningful experience. Even at a safe distance, our anxiety and uncertainty disable us because against all reason, we cannot help but to dread the absurdity of their predicament, and to wonder how distant it really is. We cannot integrate the perspective of the characters with the perspective of the viewer. There is no participatory insight or transformation. There is no meaningful connection.

3.4 The Fourth Symbol: The Zombie Apocalypse

Fig. 4: Ludwig Ferdinand Schnorr von Carolsfeld's depiction of the Apocalypse with Jesus (*ca.* 1831).[4]

Today, the term "apocalypse" is applied extemporaneously.[5] It usually refers to the end of the world, of human civilization, or a range of calamities and disasters. This is a telling inaccuracy. The definition of apocalypse as a synonym for destruction only captures one axis of its biblical origins. The Christian apocalypse was never simply the end of the world: it was the resurrection of the body, and the revelation of final truths. Just as the zombie's mug distorts the cosmos of human likeness, the zombie zeitgeist distorts the cosmos of apocalyptic revelation, by offering resurrection without rebirth (see also Moreman 2010).

3.4.1 Intensifying Meaninglessness II: The Zombie is Bankrupt; It Lacks Insight

The Christian apocalypse is the breaking of an old worldview to afford the emergence of a new worldview. As such, it represents the mutual transformation of mind and world. In the everyday,

---

4   Wikimedia, https://commons.wikimedia.org/wiki/File:Schnorr_von_Carolsfeld,_Ludwig_Ferdinand_-_Apocalypse.jpg
5   For further reading on the topic of apocalypse see also Lisboa (2011).

this transformative process refers to the shifting of perspectives to accommodate an unforeseen exposure, the sudden, spontaneous emergence of comprehensions that deepen our understanding of reality. These so-called light bulb moments are instances of "insight", and the phenomenology of this experience gives us the fourth and final mark of realness.

This mark of realness is best described as a sense of wonder. When the world cedes us something from beyond the frame of our existing perspectives, our sense of ontological surprise is deeply significant. While it is crucial for us to have a grasp on the world, it is also crucial for the world to escape that grasp so that our mapping of reality can be recast and recaptured. The feeling that there is more to reality than what we know of it strengthens its integrity, and its independence from our subjectivity makes it more trustworthy. While it is necessary, as discussed above, to feel that the world is consistently intelligible, it is also necessary to have our sense of the world pulled periodically from underneath us. Insight emerges from the wreckage of this experience. It allows our perspective to reframe itself around a fuller appreciation of reality, like stepping out from behind a camera, or losing your footing only to regain it with more traction.

The traditional apocalypse is the religious macrocosm of this perspectival shifting, but the zombie apocalypse bankrupts it. The world of the zombie decays but there is no revelation to redeem the fall. When the frame around reality is shattered, it is left asunder and never reformed. The realness marked by insight is foreclosed by the utter limpness of the zombie's world, where there is no longer sustained vitality or the ethos of industry. There is some property to this world that lacks the dynamism for creation and reinvention. Nature overgrows but nothing cultural grows from it. There is no cosmic insight that pulls back the veil on the working of reality. The zombie apocalypse breaks the world without enhancing the view, and resurrects the body without bringing the abundant life that Jesus promised.

3.4.2 The History of the Zombie Apocalypse

Fig. 5: Depiction of the Martian invasion of H. G. Wells' 1898 classic, *The War of the Worlds*. Illustration by Alvim Corréa, from the 1906 French edition of the novel.[6]

The zombie is not fiction's first instance of a secular apocalypse. It has evolved from a modern zeitgeist that has toyed with the aesthetic of apocalypse while gradually abandoning its Christian matrix. Ostwalt (1995, 2000) argues that the secular apocalypse is one that can be averted by human ingenuity and science. The genesis of this tradition was perhaps H. G. Wells' *War of the Worlds*, published in

---

6   Wikimedia, https://commons.wikimedia.org/wiki/File:War_of_the_Worlds_shoot.jpeg

1898. Notably though, Wells' novel is not completely secular; in the afterword of its epilogue, the plague that kills the Martians is declared to be the providence of God. The first true secular apocalypse instead emerges halfway through the twentieth century from deep within the wariness of the Cold War. Unlike in *War of the Worlds*, the threat of nuclear annihilation is completely manmade, and in the absence of an interloping villain, this apocalypse withholds the opportunity for any classic form of human heroism. Perhaps no film depicts this new variety of bleakness more potently than Stanley Kramer's 1959 film *On the Beach*.[7] This atomic-age story about the end of the world is one of film's first tragedies without deliverance. Crucially though, while the world depicted on screen perishes into the atomic cloud, the film retains a noble consciousness. The characters accept their fate with affirmation and dignity in their humanity. More importantly, the film arcs to a higher order purpose that transcends the frame of its narrative—it implores us, the viewers, to heed the warning of its tragedy and intervene against the corresponding threats in the real world. In its depiction of humanity, and the drive of its metanarrative (in contrast to the zombie films), the story of this apocalypse retains a vital kind of intentionality. This is where the zombie narrative differs. The zombie apocalypse exhausts the remains of hopefulness, however frail, found in these preceding stories. It is the culmination of unhallowed endings; gone is the providence and heroism of Wells, and gone is the dignified finality of nuclear twilight. As Moreman (2010: 271), following Charles Mitchell, argues, "[t]he zombie apocalypse is one that allows for the success of no human ingenuity". We have already discussed the viewers' impotence in the face of the zombie apocalypse—there is no metanarrative imperative inspired by these stories and no swell of human fellowship to offer emotional resonance. The ending is not punctuated by informed irony or moralism. It is simply the end.

---

7   Available on YouTube at https://www.youtube.com/watch?v=Ue8hC5qqMt4&list= PL_7mZVLEeOA1cJDEDL-WIZppvxBNiuSKE

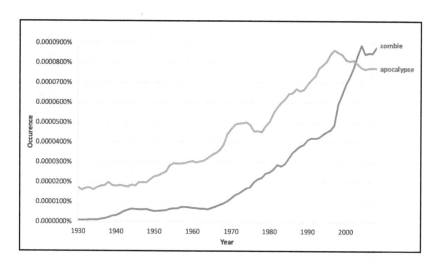

Fig. 6: The concomitant rise in usage of the words "zombie" and
"apocalypse" from 1930-2008 in predominantly English books
published in any country.[8]

As Fig. 6 suggests, the zombie and the apocalypse are independent
symbols that have magnetically found each other over the course of
the last half-century. The modern zombie apocalypse is the co-emerged
pairing of a certain kind of creature to a certain kind of world. The
world depicted within the zombie apocalypse is an analogue to the
zombie itself, causative of the creature, and created by it. This complex
dynamic has been conditioned by a generation of successive films that
have resewn the genre into the tropes we now recognize. Three of the
earliest zombie films mark this transition significantly:

- *Night of the Living Dead*—1968: George Romero's classic is the
  birth of the modern zombie proper: mindless, undead corpses
  that move laboriously and devour human flesh. Though
  radioactive contamination is implied, the cause of their
  animation is unclear and ultimately peripheral. Apocalypse
  threatens, but does not ensue.[9]

---

8   From Google N-Gram Viewer, smoothing factor of 3 (Michel *et al.* 2011).
9   Trailer available on YouTube at https://www.youtube.com/watch?v=ob8vZhSjES8

- *The Omega Man—1971*: Based on Richard Matheson's 1954 novel, *I am Legend*, this Boris Sagal film further integrates the appearance of the zombie and the event of apocalypse. After biological warfare extinguishes most of the planet's population, a plague turns a small group of survivors into a ghoulish horde of darkness-dwelling sub-humans. Here the zombie-apocalypse causality becomes more pronounced. Yet the zombification is not complete. The zombies are murderous but not mindless, anti-cultural but not yet acultural. Though it follows Romero's perversion of Christian resurrection, the film does not altogether abandon its sanctity, and ends by grasping at the symbol of a Christian sacrifice.[10]

- *Dawn of the Dead—1978*: Romero's sophomore effort gives us the first fully-fledged zombie apocalypse. By now, the nuclear overtones have faded away, and there is no exterior witness to intervene. The cause of the zombie outbreak is unknown and the fate of the human survivors, far from hopeful, is also unknown.[11]

As though magnetized to one another, zombies and the apocalypse have been drawn into an unholy marriage despite their unrelated origins. Their affinity is now so deeply cast that storytellers are hard pressed to invoke one without attracting the other, like flies to rotting food. Even two more recent post-apocalyptic films, whose conceit had nothing to do with the undead, featured startling, accidental depictions of human zombification: *The Road* (2009), based on Cormac McCarthy's Pulitzer Prize winning novel, and *Mad Max: Fury Road* (2015) both take place in a post-apocalyptic future, and although neither of these films include the resurrection of corpses, both give us a glimpse of a non-literal, human zombification—in *The Road*, the degenerating of the species into barbarous, subcultural cannibals, and in *Mad Max*, into scurrying, insect-like creatures that gather to idols of a primitive religion. The semiotic adjoining of zombies and the apocalypse is beginning to seem automatic, and emergent. The two elements couple to create a backdrop

---

10   Trailer available on YouTube at https://www.youtube.com/watch?v=NUkU18MrBzU
11   Trailer available on YouTube at https://www.youtube.com/watch?v=Yd-z5wBeFTU

genre so iconic and palpable, that to plot your narrative in the not-so-distant future of the zombie apocalypse is now akin to—and the precise inverse of—beginning your story with the line "a long time ago in a galaxy far, far away".

The term has become a common object of cultural reference that is as casually recognized as The Beatles, *Star Wars* or Harry Potter. The clime of fiction of course has a permeable membrane, and the zeitgeist has already moved beyond it. The zombie apocalypse is now the mise-en-scène for the popular theatre of survivalism and disaster preparation. Outdoor survival camps and fitness programs frequently use zombie apocalypse as their chosen terrain. Governments have even used the zeitgeist as a tableau to drum up interest in evacuation policy and disaster management procedures. Yet, the theatre of a zombie apocalypse is not so much about donning the attire of a fantasy as it is removing the attire of civility. Despite the elaborate makeup, the theatrics of zombie walking are more about stripping down the world than they are about dressing it up. There are no interesting accessories or architecture that helps to raise the pretend world from fantasy because the world of the zombie apocalypse is less, not more, adorned. The zeitgeist is altogether ugly, and that makes even the more tasteful zombie enactments an effacing kind of art form.

3.4.3 The Ecology of Worldview

The relationship between the zombie and the apocalypse is the obverse relation of a dynamical system that exists between an individual and the world she inhabits. This dynamical system is what the cultural theologian Brian Walsh (2006), following anthropologist Clifford Geertz, calls a worldview. A worldview is two things simultaneously: (1) a model of the world and (2) a model for acting in that world. It turns the individual into an agent who acts, and it turns the world into an arena in which those actions make sense. A worldview typically structures the environment to provide affordances for an agent; situations in the world are foregrounded with implicit guidance as to how an agent should address and interact with them. Meanwhile, the worldview typically structures the individual into an agent; it foregrounds and configures the behavior of the individual into coherent action that resonates with the affordances of the world. Fit together, the agent and arena mutually make sense of one another, and ratify each other's existence and intelligibility. The configuring effect of a worldview is present even in the simplest of actions: a man cuts some flowers and carries them to his dwelling. He gives the flowers to the woman who dwells there with him. Under the acuity lens of their worldview, an otherwise rudimentary act becomes the prism for a transfiguration that deepens the nature of their relation to one another. With the giving of the flowers, many significations take place: the man is transformed into the lover, she into the beloved, their dwelling into a home, and the flowers into a celebration.

The worldview is the cultural analogue of an ecology. The attunement between the agent and the arena mirrors the Darwinian fittedness between an organism and its ecological niche. A fluid worldview is akin to a healthy and balanced ecology. Just as there is the possibility for an ecological crisis, there is also a possibility for a worldview crisis. The zombie apocalypse represents such a crisis.

4. A Worldview in Crisis: The Domicide of Apocalypse

4.1 Grassy Narrows

Worldview, its creation and its loss, are immeasurably complex phenomena to chart and chronicle. Comprehending the scope and implications of a worldview crisis requires us to deviate from our discussion of the zombie and return to the work of Brian Walsh in the following section. Walsh's work scaffolds a discussion of worldview loss on a term called "domicide", a signifier for the destruction of home first introduced by J. Douglas Porteous and Sandra E. Smith (2001). In our discussions of worldview, we continue to extend the definition of home into a metaphor for the canopy of worldview, the cultural and cosmic domiciles that coordinate our beliefs and behavior, like the "faith in America" we discussed in section 2. Two case studies—one local and modern, the other sweeping and historic—will help to carry this term up the scale of magnitudes, arguing that "domicide" is the term best suited to a unified symptomatology of our meaning crisis.

Walsh discusses the Anishinaabe of the Grassy Narrows First Nation who live on a reserve in northwestern Ontario, 80 kilometres from Kenora near the Manitoba border. They were relocated there in 1963 by authorities in the Canadian Federal Department of Indian Affairs and Northern Development. Motivation for the relocation was well-reasoned; access to a variety of provisions—including schools, roads, electricity, health care institutions and employment opportunities—would be considerably improved. Most significantly, the housing that the Nation was provided with was brand new and infrastructurally upgraded. They had more power and more protection against the elements. In a very short period of time, Grassy Narrows was spared from the modest conditions of their old reserve and inaugurated into the life of contemporary suburban domesticity.

What followed was an effect that very few individuals—and apparently no one within the Federal Department—managed to foresee. By 1970, the Grassy Narrows Nation was "the site of some of the most severe social and familial disintegration, together with environmental despoliation, ever to be seen in North America" (Walsh 2006). Cases of domestic conflict, violence and suicide exploded in number, employment plummeted, welfare dependency increased and as many 1000 people showed symptoms of being infected with Minamata disease, caused by mercury-dumping upstream. "By the mid-80's, the Grassy Narrows community demonstrated the numbness of spirit and utter hopelessness that rivaled any Third World situation" (Walsh 2006).[1]

A great deal of public fallout came with the exposure of these conditions. Criticisms in both popular media and academic publications—Walsh's included—took the disaster of Grassy Narrows as an opportunity to charge the Federal Department with "cultural genocide", an accusation that interrogated the issue through post-colonial critique. Walsh noticed, however, that the deepest and most compelling aspect of the crisis was the cultural upset that occurred within the walls of the community. The transition into new housing did not have the reasonable effect that the officials in question were hoping for; even if we assume the Federal Department acted on benign

---

1   We follow Walsh in acknowledging that the appearance of Minamata disease from the mercury poisoning in the English-Wabagoon River contributed severely to the Grassy Narrows' devastation from the sixties to present day. However, Walsh also notes that the Anishinaabe attribute the beginnings of this crisis to their forced relocation, which by their accounts preceded the appearance of Minamata symptoms. It seems likely that the loss of home exacerbated the ecological devastation caused by the toxicity, undermining the social and cultural resourcefulness that would have equipped the community to respond. "As one member of the community put it, 'Now we have nothing. Not the old, not the new. Our families are all broken up. We are caught in the middle [...] between two worlds, two ways of life'" (Walsh 2006). If the dynamics of worldview sustain the coherence of family and community, the collapse of these dynamics likely precipitated the loss of those support systems; a community cannot turn to its world for help if it is lost between one world and another.

intentions, it was arguably their relocation of the reserve that exacerbated the disintegration of the Grassy Narrows Nation.

Why did this happen? Answering this question requires us to identify with a very severe kind of deprivation that occurred in the Nation's relocation. Walsh's discussion of this deprivation begins by describing a complex relationship between two interconnected sociocultural practices that, in 1963, were suddenly at loggerheads. This is the relationship between *housing* and *homemaking*. Understanding the depth of distinction in this relationship is crucial to unpacking the fate of Grassy Narrows. What precisely do we mean by home?

First, consider the role of *homemaking* conterminous to *house making*. The house maker tends to the physical construction of a space and materializes the optimal arrangement for its organization— an arrangement that precedes and afterward consummates the construction. The house is built in agreement with a design that affords this arrangement. The homemaker is ultimately responsible for it. He is the one who organizes the space long before the house maker is enlisted to raise it, and makes it meaningful long after the house maker has gone home. The relationship is effectively described by a quote that Walsh (2006) cites early in his article: "We shape our buildings", Winston Churchill wrote. "Then our buildings shape us".

Now consider the testimony of a 71 year-old Grassy Narrows elder, after his community began to disintegrate:

> We don't live like the white man, that's not our way. The white man lives close together, but we don't. We like to live far apart, in families. On the old reserve, you knew your place. Everybody respected your place. [...] It wasn't private property, but it was a sense of place, your place, your force around you. [...] As soon as they started to bunch us up, the problems started, the drinking, the violence. This has a lot to do with being bunched up. (Walsh 2006)

On the old reserve, the Anishinaabe lived in a series of circular compounds that were separated by clan. These compounds had been placed at a great distance from one another, and had equal access to the river. This distance respected the territoriality of hunting and trapping, but also helped to mark a configuration in the plot of the reserve that reflected the social structure and hierarchical organization of the community. Not only did the spaciousness of the reserve support and enable the hunter-gathering customs, but it also served as an implicit reminder of one's position in the reserve relative to his neighbors, and what that relationship permitted in terms of the cultural praxis. A clan's presence within the reserve was determined by the placement of their compound, in which the status of their membership within the culture was encoded. The particular emplotment of a family's home had significance; it gave both identity and security and told each clan where it was meant to be. It observed the sense of place described by the elder. That sense did not only connect one clan to another, but connected the reserve as a whole with the living land it inhabited. The Anishinaabe belief in "force" invokes the fluency of worldview attunement that we have discussed; there is the force of foregrounding and the configuration of place out of physical space. The elder refers to an energy that inhabits all space in accordance with a Great Spirit; even the space we assume dead or empty is filled with a spiritual quality that gives the space its vitality. Affording the place for this force was therefore a matter of necessity, tantamount to the importance of accessing water, game and arable soil. It was also believed that, not unlike natural provisions, certain places were more inherently charged with this force than others. Naturally then, the degree to which empty space could be cultivated within the confines of the reserve determined the suitableness of the reserve for habitation, and the empowerment of its residents to maintain both physical and spiritual health. It is also important to note that the circular structures of the compounds were deliberate patterns created in likeness of the "medicine wheel and the drum, and representing the four directions [...] integral to a sense of well-being, wholeness and being at home" (Walsh 2006). The circle of the home continuously impressed these directions into the cognitive landscape of significance, tracking relevant movements, delineating whereabouts and fixing the individual's position relative to the dimensions of the world around him. The old reserve of the Anishinaabe provided more than shelter. It provided a *worldview*,

> a vision of life that provides its adherents with a foundational understanding of how the world works. That means, however, that a worldview necessarily also functions as a vision for life that gives direction for normative and life-giving ways to live. A worldview shapes those who live in its embrace so that they develop certain habits [...] ways of living and relating to each other in the world. (Walsh 2006)

The Anishinaabe's home was not significant simply by its place in the outside plot, but just as deeply by the interior shape of the dwelling. It is the signifying of space that makes a *place* of it. Place emerges not simply in us, or simply in space, but in the mutual modeling that prepares one for contact with the other. Place is the way of encountering, occupying and appropriating space, the finding of relevance *within* space, and the presence of ourselves as *part* of the space. We have evidence for this anywhere we build. We build spaces that anticipate our involvement in them, and become externalized paradigms of relevance. "Buildings behave, demonstrate certain legibility" (Walsh 2006).

The residents of Grassy Narrows weren't homeowners anymore because the moment the housing project was completed, they had ceased to be homemakers. They weren't *recognizing* themselves within their homes, and they weren't *connecting* to anyone through their homes. At home, you are more than simply an occupant; home remembers you, home understands you, home is where you are recognized, home is where you belong. But recall the comments made by the elder of Grassy Narrows: the space no longer communicated to its occupants. It wasn't conveying any more. It was not telling. It was not remembering, and it was not understanding. The arrangement failed because the space was no longer phrased in any perceivable order. It could no longer answer implicit questions of who, what, where or why. The loss of intelligibility to the organization induced a crisis of placement. The residents no longer understood the affordances of their environment. They were no longer able to use their homes as a way to constitute themselves. They could no longer use them to be part of the world.

"Strip a people of that sense of place, deprive them of the space that they feel is necessary to establish such a sense of place, and they are rendered homeless" (Walsh 2006). Following Walsh's definition, the loss of home may be called *domicide*.

> Humans are animals who most fundamentally understand what reality is, who we are, and how we ought to live by locating ourselves within larger narratives and metanarratives that we hear and tell, and that constitute for us what is real and significant. When such narratives collapse, we are lost in the dislocation, fragmentation and disorientation of homelessness. [...] In short, one suffers from a worldview crisis. One runs the risk of "losing the plot". (Walsh 2006)

The zombie apocalypse is a representation of the ultimate domicide. The zombie is homeless and the exhaustion of the apocalypse renders the world unhomeable. Instead of fitting together, the agent and the arena are irreparably out of joint. Consequently, the world of the zombie apocalypse is a diseased world in perpetual decay. As Wood (2003: 105) argues, "the social order […] can't be restored".

4.2 Domicide of the Hellenistic Era

Fig. 7: Bronze bust of a man, *ca.* Hellenistic Era.
Photo by Giovanni Dall'Orto.[2]

---

2   Wikimedia, https://commons.wikimedia.org/wiki/File:1415_-_Archaeological_Mu
     seum,_Athens_-_Bronze_portrait_-_Photo_by_Giovanni_Dall%27Orto,_Nov_11_
     2009.jpg

Across epochs in history, and from individual communities like that of Grassy Narrows to entire civilizations, social order and culture appear to be universally vulnerable to the threat of domicide. Just as an ecosystem can be irreparably disrupted at any time, whether constituted by the dust mites in your pillowcase or the creatures of the Cretaceous, so too can the virtual ecology of worldview attunement unravel. That a culture is living means that, inevitably, it will die.

For instance, the Hellenistic period from the fourth-first century BCE was marked by unprecedented conflict and strife, procuring widespread social and political unrest. Alexander the Great had conquered most of the known world, and just as he was to begin his rule, he unexpectedly fell ill and died in Babylon, bestowing a tenor of senseless tragedy on an era that would incur further tragedy still. His great kingdom split into four states which subsequently went to war for the next several centuries. This period of upheaval left people massively displaced both physically and psychically. It became commonplace to be surrounded by others who did not share the same language, nor heritage, nor values. Athens had once been the seat of democracy, with every man encouraged to participate in its political and economic affairs; now, one would have been thousands of kilometers away from an unmovable, monolithic monarchy. As with the Anishinaabe, the collapse of a common social and cultural base estranged people from one another. By losing their political and economic agency, a chasm formed between people and state. By virtue of losing their connection with and being unable to act intelligibly in their world, people became estranged to themselves.

The suffocating domicide of the Hellenistic Era is reflected in the emergence of the symbol of the philosopher as physician. As Epicurus famously remarked,

> Empty is that philosopher's argument by which no human suffering is therapeutically treated. For just as there is no use in a medical art that does not cast out the sicknesses of bodies, so too there is no use in philosophy, unless it casts out the suffering of the soul. (Nussbaum 1994)

Hellenic philosophy centrally came to emphasize self-healing, in stark contrast to our zombie, afflicted by a disease with no cure.

There is something telling in the comparative semiosis of our present-day zombie and the Hellenic philosopher-physician. In the Hellenistic domicide, individual and collective agency was usurped by the widespread intrusion of foreigners and foreign rule. With the Anishinaabe however, after the initial blow of relocation, the foreignness that encroached came from within. Their worldview attunement worked against itself, alienating individuals from themselves, from others, and their cultural metanarratives. It was precisely because of the way their culture was structured that it fell apart under those circumstances, rather than offering salvation and deliverance from those circumstances. Culture amplified, rather than ameliorated, tragedy. It gnawed on itself from within.[3]

Recall from section 3.1 that the zombie eats brains—that brain is eating brain, the instrument of intelligibility. The instrument poses a threat to itself (see also Vervaeke and Ferraro 2013, *vis-à-vis* parasitic processing). The zombie embodies this hidden vulnerability twofold—it is not only parasitic on our intelligibility, but in its heedlessness it is also parasitic unto itself. It is one thing for culture to run its course and give rise to the next stage in its development, or even to be conquered by another culture—a death and rebirth, if you will. It is another for it to trip over itself and expedite its own demise—a waking death the walking dead epitomize. As Hume (1889) wrote, "the corruption of the best things gives rise to the worst". Our domicide is more like the Anishinaabes' in this sense, but as penetrating and pervasive as the Hellenes'. Therein lies the rub of the pairing of zombie and apocalypse. Nature will overgrow and smooth the jagged edges of cataclysm. Even the vampire or alien will seek to re-establish their systems and way of life. The zombie is the creature most unfit to reverse the status of apocalypse. The agency-arena breakdown is so complete, so thorough, that our very apparatuses for restoring order are themselves rendered irreparable. It is these two factors that concomitantly elevate the domicide we are experiencing to a full-blown meaning crisis. Unlike the Hellenes who found comfort from their cultural domicide in the symbol of the sage—the philosopher-physician who could alleviate suffering—our symbol of the zombie apocalypse offers only the grim prognosis that, like a cancer, our culture is doomed to destroy itself from within.

---

3   The point not being a critique of Anishinaabe culture, but a demonstration that under certain circumstances, any culture can eat itself from within.

5. The Four Horsemen of the Zombie Apocalypse: Converging Evidence for a Crisis in Meaning

Fig. 8: Albrecht Dürer's woodcut of *The Four Horsemen of the Apocalypse.* (ca. 1498).[1]

---

1   The Metropolitan Museum of Art, New York, CC0 1.0. http://www.metmuseum. org/toah/works-of-art/19.73.209/

Evidentiary arguments for the meaning crisis cannot be reduced to empirical research, though such research remains integral. It would be impossible to shed light on an indeterminate condition without venturing into territories where no present research exists. The evidence of crisis is sprawled across a spectrum of phenomena. To survey such a vast coastline, a degree of disciplinary eclecticism is required. This does not mean that our theory of the crisis is eclectic, but that to properly triage the condition, our account of signs and symptoms must vary according to the kinds of expertise required to investigate them. This suggests that an integrative, holistic approach is essential. Such is the only justification for an essay on human meaning via an exegesis on zombie lore.

However, we now have a plausible hermeneutic of the semiosis of the zombie as a symbol of the meaning crisis. It is now time to consider the empirical evidence for the existence of the crisis. While it may be possible to give a partial account for each of the individual phenomena we investigate without invoking the zombie, no such explanation can dispel the mystery of how, and why, these seemingly disparate crises are developing simultaneously and in a mutually reinforcing manner. There is, as Charles Taylor (1991: 3) notes in *The Malaise of Modernity*, "a certain convergence on themes of decline. They are often variations around a few central melodies". Although our base is holistic, we shall demonstrate a convergence of evidence for a crisis in meaning. Respecting the zombie apocalypse as the flag-bearing symbol for the meaning crisis, we propose to rhetorically organize the evidence for the crisis into categories analogous to the iconic symbol of the Christian apocalypse, *viz.*, the four horsemen. "Through distinctly Christian symbolism, the zombie can be seen to represent a subversive rejection of an enforced Catholicism" (Moreman 2010: 264-65). The four horsemen of the Christian Apocalypse—Famine, Pestilence, War and Death—carry the themes of decay and self-subversion suited to scaffold our zombie apocalypse.

If the zombie draws out our withdrawal, stands for our lack of standing for anything, and is in touch with how out of touch our worldview has become, then the zombie is the embodiment of domicide. Its lack of reflection is revealed in a disturbing trend of radical disengagement cutting across all domains of human life, deeply severing ties to ourselves, others, and an overarching social metanarrative. We stand to lose our cognizance, communicability, community and culture. We stand to become the walking dead. This is our zombie apocalypse.

We hunger for meaning in the normative void of a collapsing worldview, starving of an empty mind, facing Famine in a culture of excess. Loneliness spreads, quite literally, like a disease (Cacioppo, Fowler, and Christakis 2009), poisoning and thinning our relationships like Pestilence. At the same time, we are deeply disillusioned by cornerstone cultural institutions such as politics, marriage, religion and media—casualties of a War with (and within) the state. Death, the spectre of domicide, disengagement from our worldview, is at once the means and end, the alpha and omega of the meaning crisis that animates the horror of the zombie apocalypse.

5.1 Death

In chapter 3, we discussed the gradual formation of the zombie symbol through a sequence of films leading up to the present day. These films moulded the features of the zombie, developing the apocalypse more and more explicitly. However, perhaps the most significant property of the zombie apocalypse is the relationship it has with religion. If our culture's worldview was successfully maintained by the meta-meaningfulness of the Christian faith, the zombie apocalypse represents the death of this worldview, and the death of faith itself. Michael Walzer makes the following observations in reference to Romero's films, which, as discussed above, are the prototypical exemplars for the phenomenon:

> [Zombie] films at face value appeal to a faithless world-view. [...] Many critics have recognized the racial, feminist, anti-capitalist, anti-war, and generally anti-authoritarian stances in Romero's films. Few, if any, have paid much heed to the religious implications, however. When religion appears in these films, it is generally shown to be ineffective. (Moreman 2010: 272)

Religion is the most universal instance of worldview attunement to preside in the history of our species.[2] It is, like our individual homes, "a dense moral culture within which [people] feel some sense of belonging" (Walzer 1987).

---

2   We are not being religiously apologetic or hearkening for a return to Christian symbolism; we have no adherence to its content, merely pointing out its historical functionality.

> Worldviews—that is, these life-constructing and directing meanings—are not "ideas" that are held but "worlds" that are inhabited. Indeed, Peter Berger, would say that sharing a worldview provides a community with a "sacred canopy", a mythic cover of protection for life, under which the day-to-day business of making homes, shaping community and sustaining life together can happen. (Walsh 2006)

Consider the role of religion prior to the scientific revolution. In the West, the Roman Catholic Church was not separated from the dealings of other societal systems; its creeds and councils governed all of the systems that facilitated significant practices in society—political, economic, judicial, marital, recreational, etc. Everything was understood under the governance of the church, and it was by virtue of this overarching governance that everything came together. That is why Geertz defined religion as a meta-meaning system, a form of worldview attunement that integrates cultural relevance in all of its forms, and places all other meaning systems into an order of coherence and stability. Then came the separation: "church *and* state". A reflection of diminishment in the integrative power of the system. Broadly speaking, we in the West do not gather as a society around our churches any more. We do not rally to them for restitution. When fortuitous events occur, we do not tribute them. When terrifying events occur, we do not round on them.

In the West, we are realizing with divisive discomfort that our Judeo-Christian model of meaning, which occupied our teleological awareness for over a millennium, was unprepared for the post-scientific world into which it was ushered. In our contemporary division of the sciences, burgeoning naturalistic accounts supported by a dawning comprehension of the brain, much of our scriptural teleology no longer satisfies us to our core, and our previously personified, cooperative universe can no longer be trusted to hold us in its favour. At no one moment in particular, we as a civilization lost the anchorage by which we could govern and organize a sense of the Absolute.[3] It is an ill-kept secret that the institutions of older worlds are increasingly held in contempt, left to witness the dissenting of their congregations. In general, attendances in churches worldwide are failing despite the

---

3   In the philosophical tradition, the Absolute is a concept of ultimate reality, truth or essence whose existence is eternal and unconditional.

strained attempts of religious bellwethers to reaffirm their relevance (Norris and Inglehart 2015).

Research for the trend is piling up. According to a study by the Pew Research Center, nearly a quarter of the US public[4] and "a third of adults under 30—are 'religiously unaffiliated'—the highest percentages ever in Pew Research Center polling"[5] history, overtaking Catholics, mainline Protestants, and all followers of non-Christian faiths. This percentage has risen steeply just in the last few years, and the demographic data is telling: many of the unaffiliated in the study are identified as young adults who, unlike prior generations, are characterizing their lack of attendance in religious services as a form of disengagement reflective of their disregard. In other words, fewer people are inclined to say "I am Catholic" if they don't regularly attend a Catholic service. Instead of simply identifying with religion on a *de facto* basis (as with citizenship or ethnicity) more people are actively refusing the identification in cases where it is obviously inapplicable. This unclassifiable group has come to be called the religious "nones". In roughly half of the world's countries, they are the second-largest religious group.[6] According to the Pew Research Center, they mark the symptoms of an increasingly widespread disaffiliation from institutional religious participation. However, the religiously unaffiliated have not necessarily rejected a spiritual life. In fact, many cite the desire for a genuine spiritual life as related to their disinclination to organized religion. In other words, the refusal to invest in specific organized religions does not indicate irreligiousness. 58% of the "nones" report feeling a deep connection with the earth or nature. This finding is no different than the percentage for the general US population. Many research participants expressed the following sentiments: that though religion in general does in fact benefit society, the religions themselves are just too isolating and unsatisfying in content and in practice. In 2016, only 55% of millennials credited religious organizations with "having a positive impact on the way things were going in the country", compared with 73% six years earlier, demonstrating the increasing irrelevance and, in fact, disdain for

---

4   http://www.pewforum.org/religious-landscape-study/
5   http://www.pewforum.org/2012/10/09/nones-on-the-rise/
6   http://www.pewresearch.org/fact-tank/2015/06/22/what-is-each-countrys-second
     -largest-religious-group/

religious institutions.[7] Though fewer and fewer people identify openly with a particular organized religion, it seems that the want of a meaningful spirituality has never been more pregnant. What is clear, however, is that the spiritual vacuum is not moving people towards organized religion; it is (at least in part) causing their dissent.

In the culture of criticism, "nones" of analysis have now emerged in response to the vacuum. Many of them assemble loosely under the title of postmodernism, taking an approach to theory that subverts conventional formulations of structure, and subjects human activity to illimitable interpretability. Postmodernism reacts to the precariousness of social identity, the dilemmas of relativism, the problems of agency and the denaturalizing of mind, message, power, language and the anthropocentric world. It wonders how the individual hopes to navigate an unnavigable sea of possible meanings and whether there can ever be an essentiality to the living of life, a definitive indication of *who* and *where* we are and what we ought to be. It wonders because the answers aren't clear anymore, because modernity feels the absence of a singular governing system for our beliefs. It is as though we are struck suddenly with the realization that no one is watching us. There is no skyhook of appraisal for our performance. There is no superintendent to approve or disapprove of our actions. We have awoken to the task of being our own minders, responding to our own directives, drawing our own maps and writing our own rules. We are adolescents reeling from the prospect of our independence, disarranged from the sudden loss of a parental source. And now, it sometimes seems that anything goes. The world no longer offers itself as an attendant. All responsibility we put upon the once fated world now rests entirely upon our shoulders.

Evidence that our cultural institutions are failing us can be found in the worldwide rise of the religiously unaffiliated—these so-called "nones". Yet their disillusionment does not inoculate the "nones" from the corresponding losses of religion. They still crave a sense of home, a presence in community, and a system of shared beliefs. The lapse of the "nones" from religious participation, though different in many respects from the domicide of the Anishinaabe, poses a similar, if more gradual, declension in worldview attunement. Since this attunement is

---

7   http://www.pewresearch.org/fact-tank/2016/01/04/millennials-views-of-news-media-religious-organizations-grow-more-negative/

fundamental to the agent-arena relation discussed above, the loss has a calcifying effect on its ecology, and on all meaningful participation that was inculcated by the coverage of a sacred canopy. As Walsh and others have observed, this canopy does not simply project doctrinal and creedal beliefs, but every element of religious activity that has psychological importance; the social, communal and ritual dynamics of participating in the world beyond oneself. These dynamics are like a respiratory system for the ecology of attunement, providing fluidity to the economy of the agent-arena relation and its mutual affordances for action. In the absence of this fluidity, the ecology of the religious worldview is not sustainable. The respiratory system, without the accord of its component chambers, cannot function properly.

For the "unaffiliated" portion of our population, respiration of worldview attunement is no longer performed by organized religious influence. If the worldview of Christianity is eclipsed by secularization, then there is no viable way to recapture its potency as a meta-meaning system. This means that we need to find alternative systems of meaning that provide similar combinations of symbolic provocation, ritual and social fluency. As it turns out, such systems are not easily recreated. You cannot breathe deeply, after all, without an adequate respiratory apparatus. Out from under the canopy, our culture is left gasping in a miasma; finding our bearings in the world, establishing our capacity for action, understanding what is expected of us—these are all Sisyphean tasks while the different arenas of life remain farraginous and uncoordinated to the eyes of the agents who navigate them.

Evidence of our gasping has surfaced widely across contemporary popular culture. Ersatz mythologies have emerged as a kind of similitude for the collapsed lung of religious institutions, presenting would-be symbols of vitality obverse to the decay represented by the zombie. "A panoply of new religions formed in the wake of the [sacred] canopy's rending" (Moreman 2010: 273). Like the zombie itself, these mythologies have their origins in narrative fiction, with properties that have, in some cases, generated mass following and elevated them to the status of zeitgeist. Though they differ by source, certain elements of these fictions are concentric with the structures of the Christian mythos, and draw their significance—consciously or not—from the echo of

Christian archetypes.[8] In this way, we call these mythologies pseudo-religions; they mimic the structure of religious narratives and embody those narratives through a form of ceremonial role-play that recalls the rituals of liturgical sacraments. However, though the mythologies have participatory elements, none have espoused the complexity of belief that integrates their narrative into a fully-fledged, dynamical worldview.[9] Even while participating in these mythologies, the identification of the participants is limited, and their disbelief, while suspended, remains intact. Where a person mistakes a pseudo-mythology for a genuine religious worldview and identifies with its narrative beyond a plausible limit, his belief is regarded as infantile or delusional. At best, he is thought to be unsociable. At worst, he is considered cultish.

Fig. 9: *San Diego Comic Con* (2012). Photo by Kevin Dooley.[10]

---

8 The authors are astonished that many seem offended by the suggestion that these Ersatz mythologies are anything but secular and identify this as a 'masked man' fallacy. It would be largely uncontroversial for a cultural anthropologist to describe these activities as religious. We conjecture that these activities reflect a desire for religion, but the offense at naming them as such reflects a pervasive sense of the obsolescence, impotence and even damage attributed to organized religion. That these powerful Christian narratives and archetypes are exapted again and again through these Ersatz mythologies, however, validates some of their power and existential import.

9 Our replacement functionalities have been insufficient. They are derivative of systems—particularly Christianity—that have already been eclipsed. They do not offer something new. More than being merely derivative, however, they satisfice without satisfying, preventing the necessary transformations for addressing our meaning crisis. See also section 5.4.1 below, "Reality Disengaged: On Bullshit".

10 CC BY 2.0, Flickr. https://flic.kr/p/cxQS1s

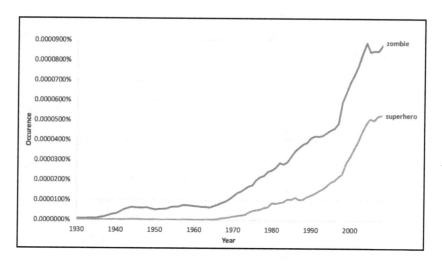

Fig. 10: The emergence of two of the most prominent modern pseudo-religious symbols, exemplified in the usage of the words "zombie" and "superhero" from 1930-2008 in predominantly English books published in any country.[11]

Modern superhero myths are among the most pervasive of the neoteric pseudo-religions. Originating in comic series in the early 1900s, their popularity has burgeoned gradually over the last half-century and—like the zombie—spiked precipitously in the last two decades, evidenced in Fig. 10. To date, there have been over 200 superhero films made by major studios in the United States, grossing over 15 billion dollars[12] worldwide and supplemented with copious merchandising. As the frequency of these films has increased, an interesting phenomenon has begun to occur; the studios responsible for these creative properties are making more deliberate attempts to establish metanarrative across the spectrum of their works. They have rolled out shared universes for their characters, with longer arcs and more integrated storylines. These are all efforts to situate the various films in a way that makes them gesture across time, makes them more relevant to one another, and by extension, makes them more intrinsically relevant to themselves. These sweeping endeavors,

---

11   From Google N-Gram Viewer, smoothing factor of 3 (Michel *et al.* 2011).
12   http://www.the-numbers.com/movies/creative-type/Super-Hero

piloted by giants like Marvel and Lucasfilm, are regenerating their popular mythos into continuous, cultural phenomena, featuring cosplay, conventions, and a cast of heroes that are as significant to many people's lives as their own professional identities and occupations.

The superhero myths have great staying power because they are practicable. Though the identification is—in the most literal terms—only in pretend, the playfulness and sense of community are manifest. Most significantly, these mythos feature figures that, like the prototypical Superman and the monkish Jedi, have unmistakable resemblances to Christ, Buddha and other divinities. The pseudo-religious mythologies have impressionistically co-opted this resemblance for maximum cultural impact. Even when the likeness is uncanny, the appeal of these mythologies is unshaken.

The internet and social media have provided new playgrounds through which to shape our involvement in these pseudo-religions, allowing people to come together under various memberships and affiliations. This is religion without existential import—its wisdom is only as good as the universe it comes from. The reasons for this are complex, and beyond the scope of this book. Suffice to say, it is uncontroversial to presume that one may live as a Christian or a Muslim, but not as an Avenger, Jedi or Brony.[13] Despite secular arguments that invoke fairy tales to argue that religious narratives are quixotic fantasies, most sense implicitly that these comparisons are wanting. The Marvel Cinematic Universe does not have equal import to a religious meta-meaning system, and one cannot simply substitute one for the other. It seems plausible however, that the rise of the former, coinciding with the decline of the latter, may be trying to make up some portion of the difference.

The pale horseman of Death rides at the axis of the meaning crisis, and the other horsemen on his flank—Famine, Pestilence and War— are variations on a sweeping cultural dissolution at the scales of individual phenomenology, distributed over social experience, and manifest writ large in the treatment of political life and institutions. In all cases, the phenomena, to the scales of each of these levels of

---

13   We discuss this further in section 5.2.3 below, "Suicide, Marital Status and Religious Affiliation".

resolution, are characterized by the same radical disengagement, the unravelling of the systems that were oriented by religious meta-meaning that is now setting below the horizon. It is important to reiterate that while each of these individual scales—we might think of them as sections of an orchestra—play a dirgeful rendition of "melodies of decline", Death provides the central rhythm. The Western decline of religion, concomitant with imitating mythologies and the growing demographic of "nones", are co-emergent with the zombie symbol of apocalypse. The many properties that constitute the Deathliness of the zombie—its mindlessness, homelessness, speechlessness, ugliness and heedlessness—are merely analogues for symptoms of domicide that have emerged along the dimensions of our personal, social and civic existence. Our horsemen are mythograms for these symptoms.

5.2 Famine

There is perhaps no greater evidence for radical disengagement from the world than the rising crimson tide of suicide worldwide. In the US, suicide rates have increased in all age groups since 1999 except those 75+, with suicide rates tripling in the 35-64 demographic as of 2010 (Sullivan et al. 2013; Curtin, Warner, and Hedegaard 2016a). Now, suicide accounts for more deaths each year in the US than by motor vehicle accidents, and is the second leading cause of death of those aged 10-34.[14]

And this isn't exclusively a North American phenomenon. According to the World Health Organization, suicide rates have increased 60% worldwide over the past 45 years. Worse still, the Center for Disease Control estimates that for every suicide, there are 25 suicide attempts. Assuming this ratio has held constant over the past 45 years, a 60% increase in suicide would suggest a 1500% increase in suicide attempts worldwide. The number one cause of suicide is reportedly untreated

---

14 Note that the increase in suicide is not simply accounted for by an increase in population or in longevity. Suicide rates reported here, unless otherwise noted, are corrected to population size (reported as per 100,000). Life expectancy in the US in 2010 was 78.7, up from 76.7 in 1999, not likely to dramatically skew the age distribution of suicide.

depression,[15] suggesting that its sufferers experience a hopelessness so thorough that the only perceived solution is to remove oneself from one's situation in the most literal sense possible. There is a deep dissatisfaction with everyday existence and a disquieting horror of its perceived inescapability.[16] Only the vacuum solution of death beckons. One is *starved* of alternatives. Suicide is *hunger* for a way out.

But a way out of what, precisely? Though we in the West tend to view suicide as a highly individual phenomenon, some of the earliest research on suicide, such as the extensive study on the subject conducted by Émile Durkheim (1897), cogently illustrates the deeply social nature of suicide and its intimate ties with a person's sense of place in a social, religious and cultural order. According to Durkheim, the horror of losing one's place in the social and cultural apparatus drives the individual symptoms of anxiety and depression that lead to suicide.

Our need for a socially and culturally meaningful life, according to Durkheim's social integration theory of suicide, resonates with the experiences chronicled in Victor Frankl's international bestseller, *Man's Search for Meaning* (1946). Frankl makes a case study for the protective effect of meaning in one's life, drawing from his many observations of the suffering endured in the concentration camps of the Second World War. The book's original German title was ...*Nevertheless Saying "Yes" to Life*, which is telling, as Frankl's exposition of an extreme loss of home, culture and community is precisely the kind of condition that can provoke suicide. Frankl's prescription for enduring involves deriving meaning from the hope that these may be restored, and that the seed of restoration already exists within the agent. His method of logotherapy gives a prescription for self-affirmation when one is "[i]n a position of utter desolation, when man cannot express himself in positive action, when his only achievement may consist in enduring his sufferings in the right way—an honorable way [...]" (Frankl 1946), hearkening back to the Stoic's response of the philosopher-physician

---

15   http://www.suicide.org/suicide-causes.html, http://www.nhs.uk/Conditions/Suicide/Pages/Causes.aspx,   https://www.psychologytoday.com/blog/happiness-in-world/201004/the-six-reasons-people-attempt-suicide

16   This is evidenced, in part, by the observation that global, stable attribution styles contribute to suicide ideation (Kleiman, Miller, and Riskind 2012).

to the Hellenistic domicide. This alternative, viable way of making sense of the world allows one to remain *at home in one's self*, in spite of external circumstances. The corollary is that suicide must not only be consequent of an agent's *hunger* for meaning; it is also the result of an inability to locate any in the arena of the world. The impoverishment of worldview engenders *famine*. Frankl himself remarks that the success of his book is not an accomplishment on his part "but rather an expression of the misery of our time: if hundreds of thousands of people reach out for a book whose very title promises to deal with the question of a meaning to life, it must be a question that burns under their fingernails" (Frankl 1992: xiii).

5.2.1 Suicide, Economic Status and Economic Volatility

One's ability to participate in a social and cultural exchange of meaning depends on a basic degree of economic agency. As such, when the economic standing of individuals or societies is threatened, suicide rates increase in turn. For instance, the market crash of 2008 saw a marked increase in suicides worldwide, mostly in European and American men aged 15 and older (Chang *et al.* 2013). In the US, the rate of increase in suicides nearly quadrupled, from 0.12 per 100,000 per year in 1999 to 2007, to 0.51 suicides per 100,000 each year from 2008 to 2010 (Reeves *et al.* 2012). Unemployment accounted for a quarter of the variance in suicide during the most recent economic crash (Reeves *et al.* 2012), and is so potent a pressure that even the *anticipation of* a rise in unemployment rate can lead to an increase in suicide (Stankunas *et al.* 2013).

The relationship between economic agency and suicide, however, is more nuanced. Durkheim's insight was recognizing that economic standing is only one of many interacting factors mediating an individual's social integration. For instance, the effect of poverty on suicide is not as pronounced as might be expected if economics alone are considered. When there is a lower class of which to speak, social integration within that class is possible, and hence the proclivity for suicide decreases. It is, in fact, individuals who face *either* the extremes of poverty *or* the extremes of wealth that exhibit an increased propensity for suicide. Additionally, racial gaps in wealth do not correspond to racial gaps in suicide. In the US, for instance, the median net worth of whites in 2014 was at least ten times that of either blacks or Hispanics.[17] And yet, the rate of suicide among whites is almost four times greater than that of blacks, and three times greater than Hispanics (Curtin, Warner, and Hedegaard 2016b). The question, clearly, is less about economic standing *per se* and more about economic *agency*, insofar as the end of such agency is social integration.

In the US, suicide rates have been increasing prior to the most recent economic crash and have continued to rise since, despite an economic recovery above 2008 levels (Curtin, Warner, and Hedegaard 2016a). Given the strong effect of unemployment on suicide, it is plausible to suggest that a perception in the faltering of individual agency in the economic arena is at least in part responsible for this suicide trend (Chang *et al.* 2013; Curtin, Warner, and Hedegaard 2016a; Hempstead and Phillips 2015; Stankunas *et al.* 2013; Reeves *et al.* 2012). Furthermore, the fact that an economic recovery has done nothing to ameliorate the suicide rate suggests that though economic *standing* may largely be restored, there may nonetheless be a looming sense that economic *agency* has not.

People have, in part, lost confidence in the institutions that are supposed to nurture both individual and collective economic prosperity. According to a recent Gallup poll in the US, faith in economic institutions is the lowest since polling began in 1973—a striking 12 percentile points lower.[18] The OECD concurs that this disturbing trend is reflected in countries across the globe.[19] The market crash of 2008, now being hailed as the "Great Recession", is a guttural example of how the machinations of large-scale institutions can threaten individual financial agency. And yet, we have little choice but to open ourselves up to vulnerability. Our dependence on these institutions is stamped into the shape of modern life, such that renouncing them is to renounce modern life altogether.

---

17   http://www.pewresearch.org/fact-tank/2014/12/12/racial-wealth-gaps-great
-recession/

18   http://www.gallup.com/poll/183593/confidence-institutions-below-historical-
norms.aspx

19   http://www.oecd.org/forum/the-cost-of-mistrust.htm

5.2.2 Suicide and Political Stability

Political volatility often interacts with economic instability synergistically, corresponding with a greater combined threat to social integration. For instance, during the reinstation of independence in the Baltic states in the early nineties, amidst massive unemployment and political instability, the suicide rate skyrocketed, reaching (and, in the case of Latvia, exceeding) 40 deaths per 100,000—more than triple the EU average (Stankunas *et al.* 2013). Political volatility in this region so dramatically saturated the pressures towards social disintegration that unemployment rate, which peaked in 2000 and 2001, had no perceptible effect on suicide rate (Stankunas *et al.* 2013). The Baltic states also suffered the worst economic losses of the EU countries in 2008, yet saw only a modest increase in the number of suicides, and still only half the peak rates in the nineties. Once again, it seems apt to say that the anticipation of agency being usurped, of losing one's place in the order of things, is fundamentally what drives the anxiety, depression and suicide associated with economic instability, an effect that is amplified if one's agency in the political arena is also threatened.

Another relationship between political stability and suicide is Durkheim's finding that suicide rates are higher in times of peace than in war, a finding that has since been confirmed in more contemporary studies of the phenomenon (Osman and Parnell 2015). War generally tends to be a collective dissent towards an external threat, and therefore demands alignment towards common goals—a high degree of social integration. In contrast, in times of relative peace, internal issues become more focal and so the opportunity for a relative loss of social integration is greater, hence the increase in suicide rate. The exception to this, of course, is war waged within a state, referring to Durkheim's point concerning political volatility and suicide.

5.2.3 Suicide, Marital Status and Religious Affiliation

The religious "nones" are spiritually hungry, but they are not finding anything to satisfy that hunger. They are the most demonstrable microcosm of the effect of worldview famine. Accordingly, suicide rates tend to be higher among the "nones" than the religiously affiliated both within a society (Dervic *et al.* 2004; Hilton, Fellingham, and Lyon 2002), and when the religiosity of different societies are compared (Stack 1983; Bertolote and Fleischmann 2002). The religiously disaffiliated also marry and have families less frequently, and tend to be more isolated from their relations (Dervic *et al.* 2004). Independently, it has been established that marriage has a protective effect on suicide (Kposowa 2000; Rotermann 2007). This suggests a curious trend among the religiously disaffiliated: they comprehensively reject or are otherwise unable to participate in major sources of social integration and meaning in life, and therefore systematically lose multiple, independent safeguards against suicide. That the fastest growing religion is no religion at all, as discussed in section 5.1, overwhelmingly signifies that religion no longer guarantees such a safeguard; its promise of a meaningful life is bankrupt. The Death of a binding social and religious metanarrative spells death for individuals.

Altogether, the rising tide of suicide may indicate that our economic, political, religious and social institutions are failing individuals, and are impotent in helping them to find their place. They fail doubly, too, as they are also unable to point to alternative viable means of engaging with the world distinct from the crumbling ones they offer. As evidenced by the rise of isolated spiritual "nones" and non-voters, people are actively dissenting from these institutions. Without one's place, and bankrupt of alternatives, hope is a luxury one cannot afford, inviting the systematic and self-reinforcing despair from which suicide can follow. As Popper (1979) said, our great strength is that we can let our ideas "die in our stead". When we are starved of alternatives, when there are no ideas left to die in us, perhaps death of the body inevitably follows. Culture, as it takes root in the individual, no longer serves to orient the agent in either *itself* or its arena meaningfully. The self is no longer at home in itself: suicide is domicide in its most interior, personal and radical form. In this sense, the zombie is suicide aborted. The seed of culture has miscarried in the zombie, and the hunger for a way out, rather than ending itself in a final act of agency, has mutated into the insatiable craving for the sapience lost—a literal hunger for brains.

5.3 Pestilence

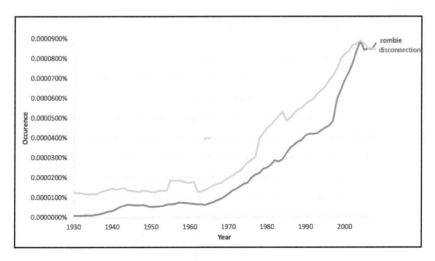

Fig. 11: Prevalence of the words "zombie" and "disconnection" from 1930-2010 in predominantly English books published in any country.[20]

Culture also informs us in relation to how we should orient ourselves to others, and critically, zombies lack any meaningful relationship to one another. People are fleeing the collapsing sacred canopies once provided by world religions, flocking instead beneath the makeshift tarps of Ersatz mythologies. These echoes of meta-meaning systems, while offering wisps of comfort, cannot afford the complete existential import of a genuine meta-meaning system. Owing to their virtuality, they ultimately fail at providing one of the central things they are sought out for—close interpersonal relationships—inflicting a myopia that seems to make people more distant to us. They are not far-reaching and general enough to make others intelligible to us across all the domains that life demands.

Evidence from the General Social Survey (GSS) paints a bleak picture of our interpersonal engagement. From 1985 to 2004, the proportion of people who report having no one to discuss important matters with nearly tripled, with people reported having 2/3 the number of confidantes than in 1985 (McPherson, Smith-Lovin, and Brashears 2006). While some have disputed these results, citing possible technical issues (Fischer 2009), even

---

20   From Google N-Gram Viewer, smoothing factor of 3 (Michel *et al.* 2011).

the most conservative modelling of the data suggests a 70% increase in the number of people who report having no confidantes (McPherson, Smith-Lovin, and Brashears 2009). As the Pew Research Center corroborates, there is "no 'smoking gun' that clearly demonstrates a technical problem with the GSS data",[21] suggesting that the backlash is at least in part as a result of the sheer incredulity towards the data. Pew also found a 30% decrease in the size of core discussion networks.

Internet and mobile phone users, however, had a more diverse (25%) and a slightly larger (12%) social network than non-users. In the UK, time spent on the internet by adults has more than doubled from 9.9 hours per week in 2005 to 20.5 in 2014.[22] This is close to the worldwide median average of 18 hours per week as of 2015.[23] Youth aged 16-24 spend more than 27 hours per week online. Given that 40% of time spent on the internet is split between social media (22.7%), gaming (10.2%) and email (8.3%), activities that are of a decidedly social character,[24] this modest increase in social network size and diversity is hardly commensurate with the effort and energy expended. That internet and mobile phone users have richer social networks than non-users, however, suggests that technology is not itself to blame *per se*. The quantity and quality of our social relationships have perceptibly suffered for reasons that seem to be largely independent from the rise in use of these technologies. The want of individuals to "plug in" and stay connected appears to coincide with the massive disconnection they are experiencing.

Marriage, as a cultural and religious institution meant to foster and protect some of our closest relationships, seems to be failing as well. According to a Pew Research Poll, while the number of marriages in 2010 decreased by 28% since 1960, the number of divorces increased by 280%. Almost a third of adults have never married, compared to half that in 1960. And while divorce is on the rise, so is the number

---

21 http://www.pewinternet.org/files/old-media//Files/Reports/2009/PIP_Tech_and_Social_Isolation.pdf

22 http://www.telegraph.co.uk/finance/newsbysector/mediatechnologyand-telecoms/digital-media/11597743/Teenagers-spend-27-hours-a-week-online-how-internet-use-has-ballooned-in-the-last-decade.html
http://stakeholders.ofcom.org.uk/binaries/research/media-literacy/media-lit-10years/2015_Adults_media_use_and_attitudes_report.pdf

23 http://www.statista.com/statistics/267518/weekly-internet-usage-worldwide/

24 http://www.nielsen.com/us/en/insights/news/2010/what-americans-do-online-social-media-and-games-dominate-activity.html

of prenuptial agreements, according to a survey conducted by the American Academy of Matrimonial Lawyers. The survey noted that 63% of lawyers reported an increase in prenuptial agreements from 2010-2013, and that prenuptial agreements have also been on the rise for the past 30 years.[25] Though prenuptial agreements are fairly rare (only about 5% of marriages), their rise may be telling of an increasing mistrust of the institution, predicated on a pessimism and premonition of failure. That we are increasingly inclined to place more faith in our money than in other persons is troubling.

This is particularly ironic considering the economic incentives for marriage. On average, the earning potential for married households is 41% greater than for the non-married. And this has actually increased from only 12% in 1960.[26] Although people are marrying later in life, and people with higher education are more likely to marry—both of which contribute to earning potential—fiscal stability is often cited as a major consideration in the choice of partner, irrespective of personal socioeconomic status.

Though marriage may be declining, the want for close interpersonal relationships and family is not. 98% of adults say family is one of the most important aspects of their lives, with 76% saying it is the most important thing in their lives. Just as we seem to be shirking from religion but still hunger for what it provides, the institution of marriage seems unable to ensure the holiness of matrimony, yet we still desire the closeness it once provided.[27]

There is a strong association between social isolation and suicide (Stravynski and Boyer 2011). Even discounting suicide, social isolation and loneliness increase mortality by 32% (Holt-Lunstad *et al.* 2015). As discussed in section 5.2.3, married individuals are also less likely to commit suicide (Kposowa 2000; Rotermann 2007). And so, we can begin to piece together a clockwork catastrophe whose ruin has been set into motion by the invisible hand of the meaning crisis. Suicide rates are on the rise. Social isolation is on the rise. Social isolation contributes to

---

25   http://www.wsj.com/articles/SB10001424052702303615304579157671554066120

26   http://www.pewsocialtrends.org/2010/11/18/the-decline-of-marriage -and-rise-of-new-families/

27   The fact that the decline of marriage is concurrent with the rise of loneliness indicates that marriage is not simply being replaced by close, non-marital relationships

suicide. Marriage decreases the likelihood of suicide (Kposowa 2000), and divorce rates are on the rise. Cultural involvement shields against suicide, and religious disaffiliation is on the rise. The religious "nones" feel that luck is more important than hard work, reflecting a damaged sense of self-efficacy and hopelessness.[28] Systematic hopelessness can spiral into depression and social isolation. Untreated depression is the leading cause of suicide. A self-reinforcing system is thereby created, the causes and effects indistinguishable from each other. They are at war within themselves. It is as though we have tools that are no longer serving us, so we are wrenching at them, turning them over, trying desperately to find a way to keep them in use, as they blunt before our eyes, and we beat them ever more harshly.

5.4 War

If suicide evidences detachment from self, and the rise in divorce and social isolation indicates detachment from others, then political disengagement indicates an appreciable detachment from the state and from political machinery. In 2014, voter turnout for the midterm election in the US was the lowest it had been since World War II. Worldwide, the picture is just as troubling: since 1945, voter turnout in democratic countries has decreased by 12% (Pintor, Gratschew, and Sullivan 2002; Solijonov 2016).

It seems that—as in the Hellenistic era—we are once again afflicted by a feeling of diminishment in our political agency, a loss of faith in the traction of political institutions, and a disbelief in the political apparatus as an instrument to underwrite the volition of society. But from here, the historical parallels are limited. While the anxiety triggered by modern Western pluralism (or in some cases, its perception) may well be compared to those experienced in the Hellenistic period, the causal parities are not nearly as obvious. This time, there is no single historical shift—even the fall of the Soviet Union, or some significant event besides—that bears responsibility for the reduced political motility, or for general agnosticism toward political participation. The diffuseness of the trend makes it more difficult to source.

---

28   http://www.statisticbrain.com/percent-who-believe-in-the-power-of-hard-work/

The circularity of the political system poses another diagnostic problem. If we face deterioration in the efficacy in our political institutions, it is simultaneous with a divestment in the belief of its citizenry. What follows, it would seem, is a loosening of the relationship between the elected and their electorate, and between the individual and the institutions to which they ostensibly belong. Though political systems do not independently constitute worldviews (in the model of the meta-meaning system, the sphere of political relations is sub-categorical to the parent function that religion once served) they do consist of an agent/arena ecology similar to that of the larger worldview. If this relation becomes unglued, then the system—dependent upon the mutual fittedness and interdefinition between the institutions and the participants—is no longer sustainable. If individuals are no longer inclined to participate meaningfully in the political process to at least a minimum standard, then the system is severely at risk of failure.

There are clear signs that such a failure is occurring, and for these we need look no further than to the centre of our modern political nervous system. In the first section of this book, we discussed the breakdown of Americanism, and the cultural discontinuities that are threatening to dilute the potency of the "American" signifier. America is the most powerful political entity of the twentieth and twenty-first centuries, and it serves as a paradigm for the health of the democratic political machinery and its requisite social capital. We proposed in section 2 that a vernacular religiosity powered the apotheosis of American identification, and that the vitality of its institutions—politics included—was linked to a "faith in America" which was at once religious and not *exclusively religious.* This faith was a paragon of worldview attunement, the hub at the centre of a moving wheel, anchoring all spokes of American life and culture. It seems reasonable to suggest, therefore, that the decline of religious participation (our first horseman) in the United States, exemplified by the rise of the "nones", has prefigured the disunion of the political agent and arena. If both losses are generalizable in the West at large, it seems plausible to suggest that, even on this scale, the two types of agnostics are co-emergent. Analysis of exit poll data for the 2014 US midterm election, for instance, reveals that although the "nones" constitute an increasingly larger sect of the population, they still only constitute around 12% of voters, unchanged since 2006.[29]

Furthermore, the growing sense of velleity in civic participation seems at odds with the advocacy-driven, often intractable politics related to our social and cultural dilemmas.[30] However apathetic we may be toward the formal offices of politics, we are increasingly politicized on the topics of ethnicity, gender, sexuality, class, and religious affiliation (or lack thereof), and increasingly trenchant about staking and defending our identities therein. It seems plausible that our elevated identification with these modalities is also symptomatic of our cultural domicide; it is a victual substitute for religious involvement, satiating our appetites for community and social coherence. In the absence of our sacred canopy, these partial modes of identification are overdrawn to meet the elements. They are exapted as pseudo-religious domiciles, shelters of culture to huddle within as we fend off encroachment by the zombies—elements of "strangeness" in the post-war world.[31]

These pseudo-religious domiciles, drawn from the matrix of social identities are attempting to cheat Death by anesthetizing the symptoms of the other three horsemen; countering Famine with self-affirmation, fighting Pestilence with tribalism, and parrying War with politicization. In doing so, they are colligating each sphere of relations through a singular framework, like beams of light concentrated through a prism.

The problem with these worldview substitutes is that they are inhibited by procrustean heuristics. Though they can virtually govern their existing denizens (advocates or members), they cannot suffice as meta-meaning systems precisely because they already function as *single-meaning* systems—they relate to one mode of identification, and they do not have the versatility to appropriate other systems

---

29   http://www.pewforum.org/2014/11/05/how-the-faithful-voted-2014-preliminary-analysis/

30   It is worth noting that the increase in protest, advocacy and intense politicization in the wake of Trump's election has not translated into participation in the actual political machinery available (i.e. anti-Trump sentiment seems not to have drawn people to the Democratic Party or otherwise resulted in the emergence of new political entities).

31   We are speaking here of the dichotomy between two increasingly contrasting phenomena: general civic apathy and politicized modes of identification. We are not disputing the existence of valid political causes or the integrity of advocacy independent from any cultural meaning crisis.

or identities. Neither do they become more complex as part of their function. Uniform collectives offer insulation rather than social exposure or diversification. Political advocacy often centers on specific topics rather than generalizable patterns or dynamics. And as would-be comprehensive frameworks, single systems are necessarily reductive; they attempt to integrate phenomena into an explanatory framework, but those frameworks have limited usefulness because they are only applicable to the system from which they originate. Like the Ersatz mythologies discussed in section 5.1, they cannot export a prescription for action that becomes useful even when placed in multiple domains or situations. The fact that one group finds a system deeply meaningful does not define that system as a worldview. It is wide and efficacious applicability among different groups that makes it a worldview.

It is telling perhaps that these modes of identification have become increasingly political when our participation in politics has declined so appreciably. We may venture to say that the politicization of social identities is a reaction to the divestment from the political process as such—a process that was once chief inheritor to the religious worldview. Consequently, it is likely that our recent divestment from politics *qua* politics is, at least in part, responsive to the disastrous outcome of the political deification that occurred in the twentieth century.

As politics is, by necessity of governance, naturally integrative of other systems, it was a proximal replacement for the meta-meaningfulness of religion at the end of the nineteenth century. Though the machinations of politics and political identification historically fell under the normativity of the religious canopy, its systemic complexity made it the nearest and most convincing imitator of that normativity as the influence of religion diminished. The twentieth century therefore bore witness to the rise of the most potent political pseudo-religions we have known in the modern world. These of course, were the totalitarian, nationalist ideologies of Marxism, espoused by the Soviet Union, and National Socialism, espoused by Nazi Germany midway through the century. Not merely instruments of governance, these political ideologies grew to espouse a creedal fundamentalism we might equate with the most zealous form of religious fealty. They were not merely inhibitive, as other pseudo-religious substitutes described above, but widely destructive. The historical conflagrations here are well known to us: though they galvanized millions of adherents initially, these political ideologies were so ill-adapted to the religious project that they conditioned unprecedented scales of violence and genocide. The horseman of War is uncannily suited to describe the fate of these pseudo-religions as they became more and more widespread throughout Europe, Asia and the Americas.

If once again we take the relocation of the Grassy Narrows as an analogue for spiritual domicide, we might say that the totalitarian political ideologies of the twentieth century were the square walls superimposed onto the circular dynamic of the religious worldview (and in this case, infinitely more overweening). Likewise, the 4th century domicide after the death of Alexander shows us what may ensue when great seats of power fail and diminish. In the wake of the last century, it became clear that if political systems aspired in earnest to a religious level of meta-meaning, they would not only be insufficient, but also inimical to our culture and way of life. It is perhaps little surprise, then, that voter turnout has declined since the fall of Nazi Germany. The notion that politics, operating as a superordinate governor, can offer anything remotely like spiritual restitution, is no longer au courant.

Though pseudo-religious nationalism is by no means extinguished, our culture's relationship to the political establishment has changed drastically since the last World War. Voter turnout rates illustrate this, and so do the prevailing attitudes expressed in our popular culture. The rabid fundamentalism of the twentieth century ideologues has, when not transferred to the social enclaves described above, largely been replaced with an obverse attitude: cynicism. Rather than the majority of individuals identifying strongly with specific political parties or organizations, many reject the pretention of any political membership at all. Like the religious "nones", the non-affiliation does not reflect an insouciance towards political agency, but merely a lack of faith in the efficacy of the existing political architecture—hence, a comparable breakdown of the agent/arena ecology, conditioned by a disbelief in the relation itself.

As cynicism is aloof by orientation, it is more spontaneous, and a more difficult phenomenon to demystify than ideological zealousness. In this way, it bears some attitudinal affinity with the decentralized, equivocal structures found in capitalist systems (see also Moreman 2010;

Webb and Byrnand 2008). There appears to be some correspondence between the pervasiveness of these two Western hallmarks, capitalism and cynicism—a sense of inscrutability, a difficulty with determining accountability, and most of all, an inability to ascertain our own influence on such a system (recall: the Grassy Narrows elder's meditations, and the Hellenistic estrangement between individual and the structures of the state). All of this conduces to a Kafkaesque sense of detachment; the perception that an individual's actions are futile in a world where causal rules are oblique. It also increases the number of unaffiliated persons as people find less and less of *themselves* in the institutions they work for,[32] in the governments that represent them, and in the monetary structures that they must use to fulfill their homeostatic needs.

Our cultural cynicism seems germane to our feeling of futility, which in turn refers us to our Kafkaesque impression of absurdity from the world outside. Accentuating this impression is the loss of some central adhesive to our perspectives; our ability to index our environment— to gain a readable purchase over our surroundings—is waning. This is because the information we obtain from the world, which becomes the epistemic leverage in our decision making, has never been more unreliable. Abundance is one dimension of this problem; one need look no further than news media to appreciate the sheer volume of (often irreconcilable) narratives that compete for authority over our attention. Far more critical, however, is the degree to which these narratives are unconcerned with their own verity, and whether the impetus for their communication has anything at all do with their relationship to reality as such (see also Keyes 2004).

This lingering question now casts doubt over the trustworthiness of all but the most verifiable assertions, whether they are made by individuals, groups or entire states. The degree to which the contents of published works, the utterances of politicians, the press releases of institutions and the opinions of individuals are rhetorically attractive is not, of course, the degree to which they are true. Yet we feel with increasing dismay that the attractiveness of our expressions is favored

---

32 In the US, employee engagement hovers around 30% (http://www.gallup.com/topic/employee_engagement.aspx), and a worldwide survey of 142 countries revealed that only 13% of employees describe themselves as engaged in their work (http://www.gallup.com/poll/165269/worldwide-employees-engaged-work.aspx).

over the soundness of their claims. The prioritization of appearance over reality, duplicated noisily in our social media driven environment, and appropriated to great effect by the political establishment, has reinforced and empowered our cynicism. Nowhere is this magnification more evident than in the rise of satirical news programs, which recapitulate political doublespeak as the basis of their comedy. Far from being persuasive, these programs presuppose the cynicism of their viewership, and this is the basis of their success. The disingenuousness of our institutions has long since been taken for granted, and on several occasions (one famous instance took place during Jon Stewart's final moments as host of the *Daily Show*) it has been given a recognizable signifier. To understand the signifier properly, we must look to a famous essay on the subject by the philosopher Harry Frankfurt: "On Bullshit" (Frankfurt and Wilson 2005).

5.4.1 Reality Disengaged: On Bullshit

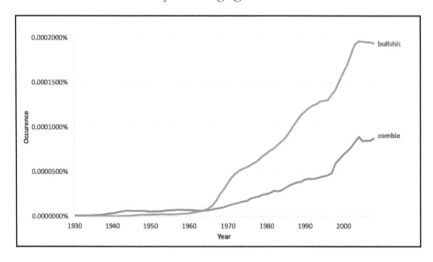

Fig. 12: Prevalence of the use of the words "zombie" and "bullshit" from 1930-2008 in predominantly English books published in any country.[33]

It is very important, in Frankfurt's formulation, not to confuse bullshit with a lie. The two differ in one all-important respect—namely, in their relationship with the truth. A lie and truth share something very significant: they share a concern for realness. The liar and the truth-teller

---

33   From Google N-Gram Viewer, smoothing factor of 3 (Michel *et al.* 2011).

possess a mutual appreciation for the depth of genuineness because in the case of both, that depth is the referent for their actions—supported by the truth teller or subverted by the liar. The lie and the truth both presuppose an appreciation of the actuality they treat. The liar must know the truth in order to identify it, and she must find it consequential for want to sabotage it. A lie is told to purposefully controvert the truth— it presupposes the importance of truth in desiring to undermine it. We might say then that a lie is told with respect to the truth. Mindfulness of the truth is essential to the projects of both the liar and the truth-teller. Bullshit is so defined because it is not troubled in the least with actuality. Bullshit may be true or untrue. Either way, it is unconcerned. It has no commitment to the truth for better or for worse. It publishes itself irrespective to the status of its own reality.

Frankfurt's (2005) theoretical explication of bullshit aids in conceptualizing self-deception far more effectively than lying does. Human beings cannot lie to themselves. We cannot know "p" and then promptly believe "not p". We cannot know we have $1,000 dollars in the bank account and then believe that we have $100,000. Even if we desire to, we cannot knowingly invert our apprehension of the truth. Lying to oneself is an inadequate, unhelpful model for explaining self-deception.

Bullshit is not about making things real, it is about making things salient. The bullshitter means to direct your attention not to the truth or untruth of an idea, but to the catchiness of an idea: a politician tells a crowd of applauding supporters that their country is the best in the world; a commercial shows beautiful women clinging to the arms of a gawky man as he opens a bottle of beer; a company changes the color of their brand and calls it "new and improved"; a student prints her essay on a smoother stationary before handing it in to be marked. Everyone knows the attractiveness of these objects is both irrational and immaterial. The crowd before the politician knows full well that their country is in dire straits but they applaud anyway. The professor reading the paper knows it is not well argued but enjoys turning the pages. Grocery shoppers can see that the ingredients of the cereal brand haven't changed, but they're tempted to buy the new box. Male viewers are well aware that holding a particular label of beer will not enhance their sexual appeal. And yet in spite all of this knowing, they are still likely to buy that particular beer. This salience slippage is not a rational phenomenon. We know there is no truth to any of these associations. Even the brands admit (and often wink at) the fact that the images most identified with their brands depict false correlations. Yet this is not scandalous to anyone because the branders are not making propositions that we consider on the basis of their being true or false. Nor, oftentimes, is the politician. She is not making an argument using the elements of reason. She is giving herself an extra sheen of salience. Salience grabs your attention, but by directing your attention, you can make things salient so that they grab your attention even more. The directives of that salience can be entirely disconnected from the depth of realness, and when this happens, you seek merely the catchiness of the idea, the person, or the prospect, and not the substance of its consequence or the reservoir of its competence. You can bullshit yourself merely by directing your attention to certain things over others, selecting certain details over others, and choosing certain expressions over others simply because they come to you more quickly… because you have conditioned yourself to favor them automatically. We can build a commitment to models of thinking and acting solely based on their salience. We can condition ourselves into retaining an idea regardless of its integrity. Our concern for relevance can come at the cost of our concern for truth. This begins a circle of self-deceptive behavior.

Bullshit and self-deception are infectiously versatile. They can be transmitted by individuals and institutions alike, and in many cases adhere the relationship between the two. As one may imagine, this is poisonous for the agent/arena ecology. If the basis of this relation is polluted by bullshit, it can have one of two deleterious outcomes. It may inspire heedlessness on the part of the agent, in which her attention becomes attracted only to salience, and her beliefs and orientations become completely subsumed into the purported appearances of an individual, institution or set of ideas. This complete surrender to self-deception makes her extremely vulnerable to ideological extremism and fundamentalism. Vigorous cynicism is the other outcome, whereby the individual dismisses herself from involvement in any of these relations. She assumes a position of absolute disbelief and forecloses the possibility of partaking in the ecology, even where it is unpolluted, and would connect her meaningfully to the world.

Significantly, these two positions are not mutually exclusive, nor as distinguishable as they would seem. Heedless belief often transforms into cynicism when a once undiscerning individual is abruptly disillusioned. Inversely, we have said that cynicism does not remove the appetite for authenticity, and in the case of political relationships, cynicism can be appropriated when it becomes its own basis for political mobilization. Ironically, devout cynicism can make an individual vulnerable to self-deception when it affectively bonds her to other, similar expressions, such that it becomes the singular criterion that guides her relationships and involvement with the world. Singular criteria like this provide dangerously low thresholds for influence and persuasion.

We are presently seeing the inter-penetration of these two forms of self-deception in political arenas around the world. Yet again, nowhere is the evidence more powerful than in the United States. The decline of the American religiosity, the disproportionately pale declarations of pseudo-religious substitutes, and the overall disbelief in the communicability of truth in politics has suffused the culture with a sense of disenfranchisement. The feeling of futility embedded in this overall zeitgeist has proved volatile, and has inspired increasingly radical demonstrations against the "establishment" *viz.* not only sitting governments or institutions, but the systemic environment (read: ecology) in which they operate. Unsurprisingly, these demonstrations have often struggled to articulate the complexity of their grievances. In 2011, the Occupy Wall Street movement declared itself against the absurd inequalities of capitalism writ large. The election year of 2016 saw the rise of political candidates Donald Trump and Bernie Sanders who, each in their partisan vestments, spoke glibly about the erosion of the American apotheosis and electrified the electorate with an uncommonly radical denunciation of the American establishment and their solidarity with the disenfranchised. Their perceived "authenticity" (whether genuine or not) has been embraced as a counterpoise to the quotidian bullshit of everyday life—a war, as it were, against the stultification of civilian life, and the rediscovery of a "greatness" that is barely recollected.

6. An Introduction to the Genealogy of the Meaning Crisis

In section 4, we discussed the modern domicide of the Grassy Narrows First Nation, and the historical domicide of the Hellenistic Era. Now, we turn our attention to a more encompassing historical domicide. The meaning crisis has its historical origins in the disintegration of three very powerful orders of a worldview that had previously helped us to make sense of the world. We provide an overview of this genealogy in the following section, reserving a more extensive discussion for a forthcoming monograph.[1]

6.1 The Meaning that Was Lost: Three Orders of a Worldview

6.1.1 Nomological Order

The first of these connections was cradled by the Aristotelean worldview, where there existed a powerful affinity between objective reality and subjective perception. This worldview had two components: an account of how the mind viewed the world, and an account of how that world was structured. For Aristotle, these accounts were integrated and mutually supporting. To know something was to understand its form,

---

1   See Mark Taylor's *After God* as a work influencing the arguments in this section (Taylor 2007).

    https://doi.org/10.11647/OBP.0113.06

but "form" didn't primarily mean the shape of a thing. It meant the deep structure that governed its organization. A bird, for instance, was not constituted by features and anatomy (feathers, talons, beak, flight, etc.) but from the underlying structure by which these features were cohered and animated. And just as hand conforms to the spatial organization of an object when grasping it, so does the mind conform to the structural organization of the world when it notionally grasps its structure. This was the Aristotelean knowing, a deep, structural conformity between mind and world.

One of the most fortifying elements of Aristotle's worldview was that it allowed criteria for falsification, a checklist for reliably determining whether or not something in the world was real: (1) ensure the perceiving organ was not malfunctioning (i.e. the quality of our eyesight), (2) that the intervening medium was not distorted (clarity of day or night) and (3) that the perception had consensus with others. Perception that passes these tests imbues *information*—it possesses the perceiving individual of the *form* of the thing perceived.

Aristotle's affinity between mind and world extended and reflected the mind's intentionality into the properties of the universe. Everything moved with purpose in this worldview, and an intrinsic sense of belonging coordinated the natural direction of all actions and objects (smoke to clouds, objects to earth, etc.). The earth was at the centre of a purposeful cosmos, an inherently beautiful and ordered place that made sense to us, resonated with our experience and gave us the sense of understanding the world and our place within it. Since it has to do with the fundamental principles by which knowledge and reality co-operate, we call this worldview the *Nomological Order* ("nomos" means law or rule).

6.1.2 Narrative Order

Aristotle's purposeful worldview was so compelling that when Christian thinkers encountered it in the Middle Ages, they found it threatening to their theology, but impossible to ignore. The most influential of these thinkers, Thomas Aquinas, worked hard to integrate Aristotle's metaphysics with important ordonnances of the Christian worldview. Yet there was an important change in the adaptation of the

Aristotelean framework. In the Greek world, time, like the heavens, was understood as a cyclical movement. For the Christians however, following the Jews and Zoroastrians before them, time was a line with a narrative, consisting of a beginning, middle, and end. Moreover, it was the unfolding of a story: the creation, fall, and redemption of the world. This metanarrative, applied to Aristotle's purposeful cosmos, anchored the affinity of person and universe to the symbolic narrative of Christ's death and resurrection. This singular, intervening event turned the repeating cycle into a single arc, creating a definite telos within a single cosmic story, and a climax for all converging purposes in Aristotle's perfectly cohered universe.

This metanarrative teleology, which we will call the *Narrative Order*, provided an overarching story into which the minutia of the cosmos—individuals and their own stories—could fit and belong. Further, it introduced the idea that the agency of persons could intervene in the cycle of repetition and meaningfully impact the course of cosmic history.

6.1.3 Normative Order

Thomas Aquinas was also instrumental to the emergence of a third order, born from a marriage of Greek and Christian spirituality. The former, originating with Plato and Aristotle, emphasized a process of rational self-transcendence. For Aristotle, "form" was the blueprint of intelligible structure for all reality's objects. The stuff that it imbued with organization was otherwise unstructured and chaotic. Aristotle called this stuff "matter"—not physical material, but pure, formless potential that was unknowable in nature. Form created a purposed reality from matter, just as a chair is made from wood that could otherwise be used to make a variety of other objects. It is the form of "chair" that fashions the object from the material. Form was the DNA that turned inanimate matter into life. It in-formed mere possibility with knowable, intelligible reality.

In Aristotle's framework, form was not simply a binary to matter, but marked a scale of being with increasing rationality, a hierarchy of complexity and intelligibility. Living beings were more in-formed than inanimate objects because their form had agency. They were self-moving. Human beings were more in-formed still, not only self-moving, but self-moving in thought—rational, self-realizing, and commensurately more real. For Plotinus, who integrated Plato and Aristotle, this rising scale of realness marked a journey to self-transcendence and realization. It reflected a fundamental desire to deepen one's connection with reality. This insight was powerful. It connected the rationality of self-movement to the process of realization: the more rational a being, the more it structurally organized itself to become more real, and the more connected it became to the structure of reality as such.

For Christian thinkers in the ancient world, such as Augustine (who read Plotinus), this pursuit of rational self-realization and self-transcendence, i.e. the pursuit of wisdom, was motivated, as Plato had realized, by a deep love for what is real. For Augustine, reason's capacity for self-transcendence was dependent on this Platonic desire, and it drove a process of ascension whereby we could transcend our reason and be in conformity to ultimate reality, a mystical union with God. Love was an extension of Aristotle's rational process, and drove the practices of reason and wisdom to form a Platonic-Christian spirituality that Aquinas was able to integrate into the Aristotelean worldview. The product of this integration was the *Normative Order*, reference to an ontological structure that connected us fundamentally to reality, and therein, in-formed us about the nature of good, setting forth a hierarchy of values that could tell us what to seek and what to love, that we may ascend the levels of reality and fulfill the potential of our self-moving, rational soul.

These three orders, the Nomological Order, the Narrative Order, and the Normative Order, became tightly integrated and mutually supporting. The story of God's love (narrative order) inspired the rational-mystical ascension to God (normative order) through the deep connection between the rational mind and the structure of the cosmos (nomological order). The world was inherently meaningful, beautiful, rational, valuable, and spiritual. We were all tightly connected to this cosmos, and we had a coherent place and purpose within it.

6.2 How the Meaning Was Lost: The Fall of the Three Orders

6.2.1 Supremacy of Will over Reason

The unravelling of the three orders is not a single historical incident, but was likely preconditioned by the Black Death in Europe. The plague created a significant labor shortage that sparked a sudden increase in demographic relocation. The abrupt trauma to Europe's social structures, combined with increased economic self-reliance, gave rise to a new sense of personal self-determination. This expressed itself spiritually as well as economically. Within Germany, the Rhineland mystics began to articulate a new understanding of mystical experience and the spiritual life. The ascent to God within the normative order was still driven by love, but it was now understood as a force of will instead of the self-transcendence of reason. Mystical experience was no longer seen as the culmination of human rationality, but as a self-negation of the will, a re-ordering of the psyche that created an emptiness into which God's will would flow. The ascent to God through Platonic love was replaced by the descent of God into the vacancy of the self, which was no longer something to be completed or perfected, but something an individual must shed to make room for the divine.

This new form of spirituality had important implications for how people of the middle ages understood God. William of Ockham and other similar-minded theologians posited that God's will was prior (and not beholden) to His reason. With Thomas Aquinas, God's rationality had been central; with Ockham, God's will was central, causative of all order and rationality. Ockham also concluded that, correspondingly, any order that human beings found in their experience of the world was constituted linguistically, and arbitrarily. This nominalism amounted to a kind of radical individualism, in which any taxonomy that arranged objects or entities (i.e. a forest comprised of trees) was a contrivance of individual will rather than a connection that was inherent to the cosmos. God's will was, above all, the determination of all order and rationality.

It is perhaps no coincidence that the emphasis on freedom and will that emerged from the Black Plague correlated with the explosion of creativity in the Renaissance. However, there was also horror in this new vision. The decentering of reason from the Normative Order meant that the mind's connection to the world had been greatly diminished. The divine had become something non-rational and arbitrary, almost absurd, and the inherent meaning of Aristotle and Aquinas' worldviews had been replaced by a gnawing sense that everything—including the self—was ephemeral, strange, and something other than we thought it to be. This primacy of the will undermined the notion of an ontological structure imbued with intrinsic value. It annulled the marriage between the rational and the mystical that had been so essential to the Normative Order.

6.2.2 Luther and the Narcissistic Self

Over a century after the onset of the Black Death, theologian Martin Luther, backgrounded by the chaos of the times, was bringing together influences from Rhineland mysticism and Ockham's theology. Luther was an Augustinian monk, and like Augustine himself, he had identified with the tremendous internal conflict and self-loathing expressed in the writings of St. Paul. Luther experienced the self-negation of Rhineland mysticism more as a self-loathing, intrinsic to a degenerate self that was both reflexively obsessed and dissatisfied. Luther wasn't seeking a mystical experience, but the same loss of self that the mystics sought to escape the narcissistic torment of their own self-preoccupation. Since the self was vacuous and self-destructive, it could not be the vessel for salvation. Any normative transformation had to be imposed from without by God's will, which was raw, non-rational, and terrifyingly arbitrary. Luther's doctrine of grace and faith was the non-rational acceptance of this arbitrary will.

As Luther's Protestant Reformation grew, much of Europe came to be dominated by these theological ideas, and they developed a deep foothold in Western culture. Faith and salvation became personal rather than collective undertakings, and individual conscience and choice became favored over institution and tradition. The mind's most secure and meaningful connection was no longer with the world, but with itself. Luther argued for a priesthood of all believers, a radical kind of equality in the church without clerical authorities. In this way, Luther's Protestantism help to prepare the way for political democracy.

For all his progressiveness, Luther's views also contributed significantly to the development of the meaning crisis. In Luther's Protestantism, the self most authentically experienced itself in the turmoil of self-loathing, and in the pursuit of God's unearned grace, His external validation. Without this validation, the spread of Luther's theology amounted to, among other things, a cultural training in narcissism; people were trained to seek external, unearned validation to compensate for the notion of a vacuous, self-loathing self. Meanwhile, Protestantism began fracturing into an ever-growing number of sects. Such expanding pluralism, combined with the radical individualism of Protestantism, meant that God increasingly became a purely private matter of internal experience. Not only did "God" refer to something arbitrary and absurd, it no longer referred to the same thing for different people. The term was starting to become meaningless.

Luther's rejection of tradition and institution meant a transference of spiritual life from the institution to the home, and into one's daily work. Consequently, the monasteries were shut down in Protestant countries. Until that time, the monastery and the university had been complementary institutions; the latter served the acquisition of knowledge, and the former was the place wherein an individual cultivated wisdom, and trained a spiritual process of self-transformation and self-transcendence. These institutions and their associated functions were complementary educators. With the disappearance of the monasteries, this balance was lost. Without a systemic way of cultivating wisdom, the growing narcissism trained by Luther's theology—now focused in the everyday practices of home, work and family in which sacredness and spirituality were now abstracted—was unchecked within the broader culture.

6.2.3 Pluralism and the Copernican Revolution

The newly integrated senses of self-determination and individualism described above helped to foster a rise in commercialism as Europe began to recover from the Black Plague. There was a prevailing belief that an individual could alter one's status through determined effort, and this belief seemed to engender increases in urbanization and trade.

By extension, this gave rise to unprecedented social diversity and created the need for efficient and impartial bureaucracies that could monitor and enforce the contracts so crucial to commercialism. The system of contracts reinforced the idea that human beings could be connected to each other outside of shared kinships or religious affiliation. Societies slowly began to become more pluralistic, and this further undermined the importance of a single order shared by all.

The engine of commercialism produced many unexpected innovations from the Middle Ages through to the Renaissance, and these innovations set the scene for the transformations to come. The complexities of long distance trading and commerce put collective pressure on the culture to develop better celestial navigation and mathematics to reduce the risk of losing ships at sea. This led to more careful collection of data about the heavens and calculations about the motions of heavenly bodies, revealing that the heavens were not behaving as predicted by the Aristotelean-Ptolemaic model. Pragmatic improvements to these mathematics inspired Copernicus' astronomical revision that the sun, not the earth, was at the center of the known universe.

The revolution triggered by Copernicus' discovery upended the presumptions of Aristotle's epistemology. It demonstrated that a person's experience could pass each of Aristotle's tests for reality—perception, medium and consensus—and still be wrong. The quality of experience was now subjective. Mathematics, not experience, was now the measure of realness and the language of the universe. If our fundamental cosmic orientation was misconceived, then everything was now vulnerable to illusion. Suddenly the mind was no longer anchored to the structure of the cosmos, and Aristotle's nomological order could no longer be trusted to keep us in conformity with the world.

Galileo took Copernicus' revolution even further with his discovery of inertial motion, which revealed that things did not move because of an internal purpose or cosmic drive, but because of accidental external pushes from other, unintentional forces in the world. The loss of these drives implied that here was no overarching metanarrative at work within the cosmos, no story that enacted itself through the movements of objects and individuals. This meant that human beings were now strangers, alone with our intent, acting with determined purpose in a world that fundamentally lacked it. The universe went from being a beautiful, living cosmos unfolding a great story to a lifeless series of random collisions signifying nothing.

The dissonance between the human being's experience of meaning and the purposeless vacuum introduced by Copernicus and Galileo's discoveries inevitably interacted with Luther's narcissistic self and arbitrary God. In consequence, the mind's connection to reality—and the people and objects within it—was severed and the mind was trapped inside the illusion of its own experience. With the discovery of inertial motion, it became clear that matter was not the potential for form, but substance in its own right. Form was not, after all, the blueprint for cosmic purpose, but simply the result of how motion shaped matter. There was no value-based hierarchy governing reality any more than there was a great narrative to guide it. So there was no longer a nomological order uniting the mind to the world, no overarching narrative order providing the purpose for it all, and no normative order for ascending to the divine.

The historical domicide described within the loss of these three orders represents a comprehensive breakdown of the agent-arena correspondence discussed in section 3.4.3, which is essential to creating and sustaining a worldview. Therefore, the symbol of the zombie apocalypse, elucidated by our four horsemen of the apocalypse (section 5), exemplifies the loss of these orders in its portrayal of the "Gray Life" of the meaning crisis.

7. Conclusion

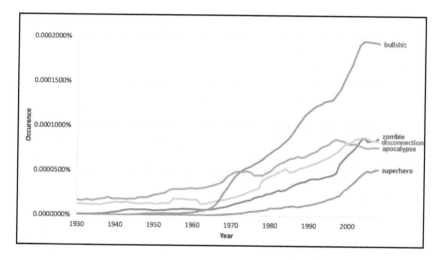

Fig. 13: Prevalence of words from 1930-2010 in predominantly English books published in any country.[1]

Our four horsemen of the apocalypse are, like the zombie itself, mythograms for a crisis in meaning that is decentered from any particular object or symptom that may refer back to it. Just like our present ecological crisis, there is no single anthropogenic or historical cause; rather, it is emergent from the unpredictable combinations of historical and perennial forces that define the interactional tension between agent and arena. As such, there is no "silver technological bullet" to solve our ecological crisis, nor stake to vanquish our zombie apocalypse. It

---

1   From Google N-Gram Viewer, smoothing factor of 3 (Michel *et al.* 2011).

is important to understand the implications of this. Responding to such an emergent problem is not simply a matter of doctoring. Communities of intelligent people can combine knowledge to triage problems in medicine, economics, and engineering, but resolving the problems discussed in the second half of this book requires more than simply pooling knowledge and resources; the solution, like the problem, must be more complex than the sum of these parts.

The problem seems sufficiently nebulous that we cannot ruminate our way out of it, and while it is not our intention to foreclose the possibilities that human ingenuity might bring to bear, the problem is likely too multifarious to be treated with any existing cultural apparatus. As we have argued, the only apparatus that provided a comprehensive worldview attunement—which could both empower and connect the arenas of individual, social, spiritual and political life in the way that we crave—is no longer a live option for us.

It is not controversial to note that the features of our Christian worldview are the prime movers behind many of our cultural zeitgeists. If this is true, it is also likely that the rising popularity of the superhero myths and similar trends reflect an unconscious response to the loss of that worldview. These mythologies, as we have discussed, contain unmistakable recursions to Christian forms, and that these mythologies are so culturally powerful may suggest that our need for a religious worldview retains a powerful hold over us. Despite our increasing skepticism and secularity, we are continually referring back to our most known spiritual quantity. This paradox reveals a complicated tension: our research demonstrates that we are increasingly—and perhaps irreversibly—abdicating religious institutions, but our cultural mythologies depict us ever more desperately beholden to religious meanings. This tension is embodied in the religious "nones" who hang ambiguously between secular and religious identities, wanting for something that integrates and transcends the realness of both of these perspectives.

A worldview that governed perspective for two millennia does not simply vanish. Its decline is gradual like that of many lesser empires. Its continued influence through the kaleidoscope of popular culture is a trailing therapy to disarm the nihilism of a secularizing world. Yet it is doomed to fail in this role. These mythologies that refer to

Christianity contain little that is new or revelatory, and their gesturing has an inert effect rather than a transcendent one. If this crisis has in part been induced by the decline of Christianity, then attempting to retrieve Christianity is an ill-fated attempt at a solution. The very hard problem is this: that we suffer a lack of viable alternatives. As we have discussed, twentieth century solutions to the problem of religious decline have resulted in the trauma of disastrous political ideologies. We are rightly wary of duplicating this result with another secular attempt at worldview attunement. Absent these meta-meaning systems—one diminishing, and the other counterfeit—the only alternative seems to be the raw domicide of nihilism.

The impasse posed by this trilemma is a spiritual bankruptcy that cannot be thwarted by the benefit of historical hindsight; our only known cure for cultural domicide—the one that relieved the Hellenes—is now at the very centre of the ailment. The philosopher-as-physician was the fountainhead of Christianity's spiritual framework, and our divestment from this framework foregrounds our current predicament. It remains unclear to what extent, and in what form, this framework can be salvaged in a secular world, and this is the most significant formulation of the problem we face as a society. This unanswered question, while outside the scope of this discussion, will be the subject of the authors' forthcoming work.

Our spiritual bankruptcy, deepened and exacerbated by the symptoms of crisis in each of our horseman's domains, are symbolized powerfully by the zombie apocalypse: by the vapid environment, the craving monster, the perverted transformation of world, the lack of instructive precedent, and the absence of an apparatus to treat or to explain. The growing recognition that there is no single technological solution to the environmental crisis corresponds to the lack of stake or silver bullet for a zombie apocalypse. The semiosis of the zombie's physicality, the ambiguity around its name and iconicity, its subversion of archetypally heroic narratives and its undermining of our purchase on realness: all of this serves to make the zombie an exegetically polymorphic monster—a versatile symbol for despair, decay and faithlessness. That the zombie's myth centers on the abjection of Christian apocalypse and resurrection suggests that its evolution is culturally responsive to the eclipse of the religious worldview, reflecting a loss of normative agency and emblematizing the estrangement of individuals from one another and the infertility of their ecology with the world.

It is important for the authors to stress that we are not resigned to the nihilism described in this book. To say that a problem is not easily solved is not to say that it is unsolvable. Rather, the purpose of this work has been to articulate the ways in which the symbol of this prominent cultural zeitgeist correlate to the decline of the Christian worldview, and to the many forms of crises that seem in turn connected to this decline. It remains imperative not to permit the voguishness of the zombie zeitgeist to undermine its philosophical import when appreciating the impact of a crisis in meaning, nor to reductively attribute the zeitgeist to any single horseman of crisis discussed in this book. The effects of both the Grassy Narrows and Hellenistic domicides discussed in section 4 adduce the gravity of consequence that follows the disintegration of a meta-meaning system. A comparable disintegration is extant; the zombie is a multi-vocal analogue for the contemporaneous domicides occurring in the personal, social, political and spiritual systems of the present. We may speculate without great imagination that this gradual onslaught of meaninglessness will—in the absence of a new sacred canopy—continue to threaten and infect us for the foreseeable future.[2]

---

2   This book is situated within a more encompassing argument, presented in *Buddhism and Cognitive Science: Responding to the Meaning Crisis*, University of Toronto. Available on YouTube at https://www.youtube.com/watch?v=Uc8wy_4H8X8

References

Bertolote, José Manoel, and Alexandra Fleischmann. 2002. "A Global Perspective in the Epidemiology of Suicide", *Suicidologi*, 7: 6–8. http://iasp.info/pdf/papers/Bertolote.pdf

Cacioppo, John T., James H. Fowler, and Nicholas A. Christakis. 2009. "Alone in the Crowd: The Structure and Spread of Loneliness in a Large Social Network", *Journal of Personality and Social Psychology*, 97: 977–91, https://doi.org/10.1037/a0016076

Chang, Shu-Sen, David Stuckler, Paul Yip, and David Gunnel. 2013. "Impact of 2008 Global Economic Crisis on Suicide: Time Trend Study in 54 Countries", *British Medical Journal*, 347: f5239, https://doi.org/10.1136/bmj.f5239

Curtin, Sally C., Margaret Warner, and Holly Hedegaard. 2016a. "Increase in Suicide in the United States, 1999-2014", NCHS data brief, no 241: 1–8, https://www.ncbi.nlm.nih.gov/pubmed/27111185

—. 2016b. "Suicide Rates for Females and Males by Race and Ethnicity: United States, 1999 and 2014", National Center for Health Statistics Health E-Stat, https://www.cdc.gov/nchs/data/hestat/suicide/rates_1999_2014.pdf

Deleuze, G., and F. Guattari. 1972. *Anti-Oedipus: Capitalism and Schizophrenia* (University of Minnesota Press: Minneapolis).

Dervic, Kanita, Maria A. Oquendo, Michael F. Grunebaum, Steve Ellis, Ainsley K. Burke, and J. John Mann. 2004. "Religious Affiliation and Suicide Attempt", *The American Journal of Psychiatry*, 161: 2303–08, https://doi.org/10.1176/appi.ajp.161.12.2303

Dreyfus, Hubert, and Sean Dorrance Kelly. 2011. *All Things Shining: Reading the Western Classics to Find Meaning in a Secular Age* (Simon and Schuster: New York).

Durkheim, Émile. 1897. *Le Suicide: Étude De Sociologie* (Alcan: Paris), http://classiques.uqac.ca/classiques/Durkheim_emile/suicide/suicide.html

Fischer, Claude S. 2009. "The 2004 GSS Finding of Shrunken Social Networks: An Artifact?", *American Sociological Review*, 74: 657–69, https://doi.org/10.1177/000312240907400408

Frankfurt, Harry G., and George Wilson. 2005. *On Bullshit* (Princeton University Press: Princeton).

Frankl, Victor Emil. 1946. …*Trotzdem Ja Zum Leben Sagen: Ein Psychologe Erlebt Das Konzentrationslager* (Verlag für Jugend und Volk: Vienna).

—. 1992. *Man's Search for Meaning* (Beacon Press: Boston).

Goto-Jones, Christopher S. 2015. "Zombie Apocalypse as Mindfulness Manifesto (after Žižek)", *Postmodern Culture*, 24, https://doi.org/10.1353/pmc.2013.0062

Hempstead, Katherine A., and Julie A. Phillips. 2015. "Rising Suicide among Adults Aged 40-64 Years: The Role of Job and Financial Circumstances", *American Journal of Preventive Medicine*, 48: 491–500, https://doi.org/10.1016/j.amepre.2014.11.006

Hilton, Sterling C., Gilbert W. Fellingham, and Joseph L. Lyon. 2002. "Suicide Rates and Religious Commitment in Young Adult Males in Utah", *American Journal of Epidemiology*, 155: 413–19, https://doi.org/10.1093/aje/155.5.413

Holt-Lunstad, Julianne, Timothy B. Smith, Mark Baker, Tyler Harris, and David Stephenson. 2015. "Loneliness and Social Isolation as Risk Factors for Mortality", *Perspectives on Psychological Science*, 10: 227–37, https://doi.org/10.1177/1745691614568352

Hume, David. 1889. *The Natural History of Religion* (A. and H. Bradlaugh Bonner: London), http://oll.libertyfund.org/titles/hume-the-natural-history-of-religion

Huxley, Aldous. 1962. *Island* (Bantam Books: New York).

Keyes, Ralph. 2004. *The Post-Truth Era: Dishonesty and Deception in Contemporary Life* (St. Martin's Press: New York).

Kleiman, Evan M., Adam B. Miller, and John H. Riskind. 2012. "Enhancing Attributional Style as a Protective Factor in Suicide", *Journal of Affective Disorders*, 143: 236–40, https://doi.org/10.1016/j.jad.2012.05.014

Kposowa, Augustine J. 2000. "Marital Status and Suicide in the National Longitudinal Mortality Study", *Journal of Epidemiology and Community Health*, 54: 254–61.

Lisboa, Maria Manuel. 2011. *The End of the World: Apocalypse and its Aftermath in Western Culture* (Open Book Publishers: Cambridge), http://www.openbookpublishers.com/product/106

McPherson, Miller, Lynn Smith-Lovin, and Matthew E. Brashears. 2006. "Social Isolation in America: Changes in Core Discussion Networks over Two Decades", *American Sociological Review*, 71: 353–75, https://doi.org/10.1177/000312240607100301

—. 2009. "Reply to Fischer: Models and Marginals: Using Survey Evidence to Study Social Networks", *American Sociological Review*, 74: 670–81, https://doi.org/10.1177/000312240907400409

Michel, Jean-Baptiste, Yuan Kui Shen, Aviva Presser Aiden, Adrian Veres, Matthew K. Gray, Joseph P. Pickett, Dale Hoiberg, Dan Clancy, Peter Norvig, Jon Orwant, Steven Pinker, Martin A. Nowak, and Erez Lieberman Aiden. 2011. "Quantitative Analysis of Culture Using Millions of Digitized Books", *Science*, 331: 176–82, https://doi.org/10.1126/science.1199644

Moreman, Christopher M. 2010. "Dharma of the Living Dead: A Meditation on the Meaning of the Hollywood Zombie", *Studies in Religion*, 39: 263–81, https://doi.org/10.1177/0008429810362316

Norris, Pippa, and Ronald Inglehart. 2015. "Are High Levels of Existential Security Conducive to Secualization? A Response to Our Critics". In Stanley D. Brunn (ed.), *The Changing World Religion Map: Sacred Places, Identities, Practices and Politics* (Springer Science+Business Media: Dordrecht), https://doi.org/10.1007/978-94-017-9376-6_177

Nussbaum, Martha C. 1994. "Therapeutic Arguments". In her *The Therapy of Desire: Theory and Practice in Hellenistic Ethics* (Princeton: Princeton University Press).

Osman, Mugtaba, and Andrew C. Parnell. 2015. "Effect of the First World War on Suicide Rates in Ireland: An Investigation of the 1864-1921 Suicide Trends", *British Journal of Psychiatry Open*, 1: 164–65, https://doi.org/10.1192/bjpo.bp.115.000539

Ostwalt, Conrad E. 1995. "Hollywood and Armageddon: Apocalyptic Themes in Recent Cinematic". In J. W. Martin and C. E. Ostwalt (eds.), *Screening the Sacred* (Westview Press: Oxford).

—. 2000. "Armageddon at the Millennial Dawn", *The Journal of Religion and Film*, 1.4, http://digitalcommons.unomaha.edu/jrf/vol4/iss1/4

Pintor, Rafael López, Maria Gratschew, and Kate Sullivan. 2002. "Voter Turnout Rates from a Comparative Perspective". In Rafael López Pintor and Maria Gratschew (eds.), *Voter Turnout since 1945: A Global Report* (Bulls Press: Halmstad, Sweden).

Popper, Karl Raimund. 1979. *Objective Knowledge: An Evolutionary Approach* (Clarendon Press: Oxford).

Porteous, Douglas, and Sandra E. Smith. 2001. *Domicide: The Global Destruction of Home* (McGill-Queen's University Press: Kingston).

Reeves, Aaron, David Stuckler, Martin McKee, David Gunnell, Shu-Sen Chang, and Sanjay Basu. 2012. "Increase in State Suicide Rates in the USA During Economic Recession", *The Lancet*, 380, https://doi.org/10.1016/S0140-6736(12)61910-2

Rotermann, M. 2007. "Marital Breakdown and Subsequent Depression", Health Reports, 18: 33–44, http://www.statcan.gc.ca/pub/82-003-x/2006005/article/marital-conjugal/9636-eng.pdf

Solijonov, Abdurashid. 2016. Voter Turnout Trends Around the World (IDEA: Stockholm), http://www.idea.int/publications/catalogue/voter-turnout-trends-around-world?lang=en

Stack, Steven. 1983. "The Effect of Religious Commitment on Suicide: A Cross-National Analysis", *Journal of Health and Social Behavior*, 24: 362–74, https://doi.org/10.2307/2136402

Stankunas, Mindaugas, Jutta Lindert, Mark Avery, Ros Sorensen, Konstantinos N. Fountoulakis, Sotirios A. Koupidis, Melina Siamouli, Ilias A. Grammatikopoulos, and Pavlos N. Theodorakis. 2013. "Suicide, Recession, and Unemployment", *The Lancet*, 381: 721–22, https://doi.org/10.1016/S0140-6736(13)60572-3

Stravynski, Ariel, and Richard Boyer. 2011. "Loneliness in Relation to Suicide Ideation and Parasuicide: A Population-Wide Study", *Suicide and Life-Threatening Behavior*, 31: 32–40, https://doi.org/10.1521/suli.31.1.32.21312

Sullivan, Erin M., Joseph L. Annest, Feijun Luo, Thomas R. Simon, and Linda L. Dahlberg. 2013. "Suicide among Adults Aged 35-64 Years — United States, 1999-2010", Morbidity and Mortality Weekly Report, 62: 321–25, https://www.cdc.gov/mmwr/preview/mmwrhtml/mm6217a1.htm

Taylor, Charles. 1991. *The Malaise of Modernity* (House of Anasi Press: Toronto).

Taylor, Mark C. 2007. *After God* (University of Chicago Press: Chicago).

Vervaeke, John, and Leonardo Ferraro. 2013. "Relevance, Meaning and the Cognitive Science of Wisdom". In Michel Ferrari and Nic M. Weststrate (eds.), *The Scientific Study of Personal Wisdom: From Contemplative Traditions to Neuroscience* (Springer Netherlands: Dordrecht), https://doi.org/10.1007/978-94-007-7987-7_2

Walsh, Brian. 2006. "From Housing to Homemaking: Worldview and the Shaping of Home", *Christian Scholar's Review*, 35: 237–57.

Walzer, Michael. 1987. *Interpretation and Social Criticism* (Harvard University Press: Cambridge).

Webb, Jen, and Sam Byrnand. 2008. "Some Kind of Virus: The Zombie as Body and as Trope", *Body and Society*, 14: 83–98, https://doi.org/10.1177/1357034X08090699

Wood, R. 2003. *Hollywood from Vietnam to Reagan... and Beyond* (Columbia University Press: New York).

Index

This book need not end here...

At Open Book Publishers, we are changing the nature of the traditional academic book. The title you have just read will not be left on a library shelf, but will be accessed online by hundreds of readers each month across the globe. OBP publishes only the best academic work: each title passes through a rigorous peer-review process. We make all our books free to read online so that students, researchers and members of the public who can't afford a printed edition will have access to the same ideas.

This book and additional content is available at:
https://www.openbookpublishers.com/product/590

Customize

Personalize your copy of this book or design new books using OBP and third-party material. Take chapters or whole books from our published list and make a special edition, a new anthology or an illuminating coursepack. Each customized edition will be produced as a paperback and a downloadable PDF. Find out more at:
https://www.openbookpublishers.com/section/59/1

Donate

If you enjoyed this book, and feel that research like this should be available to all readers, regardless of their income, please think about donating to us. We do not operate for profit and all donations, as with all other revenue we generate, will be used to finance new Open Access publications.
https://www.openbookpublishers.com/section/13/1/support-us

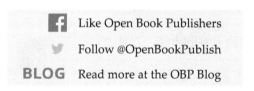

f   Like Open Book Publishers

🐦   Follow @OpenBookPublish

BLOG   Read more at the OBP Blog

You may also be interested in:

The End of the World
Apocalypse and its Aftermath in Western Culture

By Maria Manuel Lisboa

https://www.openbookpublishers.com/product/106

God's Babies
Natalism and Bible Interpretation in Modern America

By John McKeown

https://www.openbookpublishers.com/product/263

The Altering Eye
Contemporary International Cinema

By Robert Phillip Kolker

https://www.openbookpublishers.com/product/8